OXFORD
UNIVERSITY PRESS

ASPIRE
SUCCEED
PROGRESS

exam SUCCESS

in

ENGLISH AS A SECOND LANGUAGE

for Cambridge IGCSE®

Brian Dyer
Dean Roberts

Oxford excellence for

OXFORD

UNIVERSITY PRESS

Great Clarendon Street, Oxford, OX2 6DP, United Kingdom

Oxford University Press is a department of the University of Oxford. It furthers the University's objective of excellence in research, scholarship, and education by publishing worldwide. Oxford is a registered trade mark of Oxford University Press in the UK and in certain other countries

British Library Cataloguing in Publication Data
Data available

978 0 19 839609 3

1 3 5 7 9 10 8 6 4 2

Paper used in the production of this book is a natural, recyclable product made from wood grown in sustainable forests. The manufacturing process conforms to the environmental regulations of the country of origin.

Printed in Great Britain by Bell and Bain, Ltd. Glasgow

Acknowledgements
The publishers would like to thank the following for permissions to use their photographs:

Cover: Shutterstock

Artwork by Aptara Inc.

Although we have made every effort to trace and contact all copyright holders before publication this has not been possible in all cases. If notified, the publisher will rectify any errors or omissions at the earliest opportunity.

Links to third party websites are provided by Oxford in good faith and for information only. Oxford disclaims any responsibility for the materials contained in any third party website referenced in this work.

Contents

Introduction

This book aims to give you practice for all three examination papers, covering all four main skills:

1. Reading:
   - to locate specific details
   - to understand and get the gist of an article
   - to make notes
   - to write a summary
   - to use scanning skills.

2. Writing:
   - to produce a short summary
   - to turn your notes into a longer piece of writing
   - to produce extended pieces using different registers and for different purposes.

3. Listening:
   - to identify specific detail
   - to understand a speaker's gist
   - to work out a speaker's views and opinions.

4. Speaking:
   - to prepare for and take part in a two-way, fluent discussion about a given topic.

Content and themes

When you take your final examination, you will cover a broad range of themes and topics. We have decided to focus each paper on the following themes, but each theme could appear anywhere in any of the three examinations you will take:

Paper 1: science, technology, travel, transport, communication

Paper 2: food, fitness, health, hobbies, interests, leisure

Paper 3: animals, working life, entertainment, festivals, outdoor activities

Paper 4: global issues, customs, cultures, communities, past and future.

We believe that the four papers cover all of the standard topics and themes that you will have learned about on your IGCSE® course and will therefore prepare you effectively for the content element of the examination.

Structure of the book

There are four full examination papers. We recommend you work through each paper in order, from Paper 1 to Paper 4.

The first two papers provide a lot of guidance to help you familiarise yourself with the exams but also to give hints and tips to help you achieve greater success. We have done this using three feature boxes:

> ✓ **Preparing for the question**
> Here, we point out the key skills being tested, and give you some examples of the types of responses that are required.

Study tips

Here, we provide a range of responses, some of which are correct, others which are not correct or perhaps need further information. We guide you through these with advice about the detail and precision of the required response.

 Self-assessment

When you mark your own answers using the detailed answer grids we have provided, you can also refer to this section where we explain why some answers are correct and others might not be. This should help you mark your own work confidently and accurately.

The third and fourth papers are full, authentic practice exams and do not contain any guidance or input from us. You can use these as revision and you can complete a full paper, or perhaps divide the paper into sections or questions so you can practise a particular skill.

Answer grids, mark schemes and evaluating your progress

We have made this as detailed as possible and some answer grids also contain advice about how to improve your skills in providing succinct and accurate responses. Some grids contain answers that would not be acceptable, for example.

You can mark your own work using the mark schemes provided, which means you can arrive at a total score for a section or indeed for a full examination paper. We have also provided a means for you to evaluate your progress for reading, writing, listening and speaking.

By the end of the first two papers you should have a good idea of your strengths and weaknesses and you can use this evaluation to do any preparation work before you attempt the full Paper 3 and 4.

The approach we have taken for Speaking

To help you practise for your Oral Test, we have included four practice Oral Test cards which follow the same format as the examination paper. We have also recorded part of the discussions so that you can practise the key skill of developing your fluency in the context of a semi-formal conversation. You will hear a series of questions and prompts that your teacher might ask you and you will have the chance to respond at your own pace. We hope that this will strengthen your speaking skills, and also your listening skills!

A brief note for Core level students

This book has been designed for the Extended level examination papers. However, this does not mean that a student who will take the Core level papers cannot use the book. Quite the opposite; we feel that many of the exercises, questions and skills that are practised are very useful for the Core level student to help build up knowledge and confidence. The mechanism we use to calculate total marks is however based on the Extended papers, so we advise Core level students to ignore this and use this resource for familiarisation and practice-only purposes. The key skills are almost the same for both levels, but the content in this book has been aimed at the higher level.

Get familiar with the examination
Paper 1 Reading and writing
Overview of the exercises

When you work through this practice examination paper you will be able to give yourself marks for each exercise. The table below shows the total number of marks you can get for each exercise. You can add up your marks to arrive at totals for your reading and your writing skills. You should be able to see which skill is your strongest and where you need to improve. You can then arrive at a total mark out of 80.

	Marks for reading	Marks for writing
Exercise 1: Reading	13	0
Exercise 2: Multiple matching	10	0
Exercise 3: Note making	9	0
Exercise 4: Summary	8	8
Exercise 5: Writing	0	16
Exercise 6: Writing	0	16
Total marks	**40**	**40**

Now use the table below to see how well you have done.

Mark	Comment
67 marks and over	Excellent and things are looking great for a top grade in your examination.
51 to 66 marks	Good, you should be heading for a solid performance and a good grade in your exam.
39 to 50 marks	You can be happy with this score, but there are clearly some areas you need to review where you could improve and pick up more marks. However, you are heading for a satisfactory grade.
28 to 49 marks	There are clearly some weak areas or problem areas where you are losing marks, but don't panic: this is practice and you probably need more practice. We think it would be useful to get some advice and guidance from a teacher, parent or friend, so that you can see where you need to improve.
Below 28 marks	We don't think you are ready to take this examination and we advise you to practise more to develop your English. You will probably need more classroom time learning English and it would also be useful to use English outside of the classroom as much as you can.

EXERCISE 1 • Reading	
Type of task:	This is a reading exercise. You will read a text which will test your scanning skills. For your answers, you do not need to write full sentences, short responses are sufficient. You will have to understand what the writer of the text has implied as well as factual details. The format will be either a report or newspaper/magazine article.
You will be assessed on:	• identifying and retrieving facts and details • recognising and selecting relevant information • understanding what is implied in the text, such as the writer's feelings or opinions
Number of questions and marks:	There are 9 questions worth 13 marks in total. The last question (question (i)) asks you to scan the article with a main theme or idea in mind and find four details, worth 1 mark each, so a total of 4 marks can be achieved. Total of 13 marks

---

✔ Preparing for the question

Scanning is an important skill here, so read through the article quickly to try and find a key word or phrase in a question that matches a point in the text. Key words will show you where to look in the text for your answers. For example, in question (g) the key word is *observe* but in the text it is *noticed*.

Try to work through the questions from (a) to (i) in sequence because they are usually in the same order as the information in the text. Remember also that the final question carries 4 marks and the information can be from anywhere in the text, so be prepared to look through the whole article again to find the answers.

Focus on vocabulary

	Word as used in article	Usage in other contexts
cut out	*the engine cut out*	The motor cut out and the machine stopped working.
unfavourable	*the weather had been particularly unfavourable*	The rain and strong wind meant that the open-air concert had to be cancelled.
propellor	*the aircraft's propeller was broken*	Before the invention of jet engines, aircraft were driven by propellers that turned at incredible speed.
pioneered	*they pioneered an industry*	They were the first to discover the idea and pioneered the process through its early stages.

 **Exercise 1**

Read the following article, and then answer the questions.

A landmark in aviation history

In 1904, the American Wilbur Wright became the first person to fly an aircraft and stay in the air for more than five minutes. However, aviation was developing very fast at that time and only five years later, in 1909, the Frenchman Louis Blériot made the first cross-Channel flight of about 45 kilometres between Calais (in France) and Dover (in England).

Louis Blériot was a French aviator, inventor and engineer and had become very interested in flying aircraft while he was at school. He first decided to experiment with aircraft design, after seeing an exhibition of flight at a World Fair in Paris. For about eight years he experimented with several designs and escaped from two serious air crashes with relatively minor injuries. On one occasion, his aircraft was flying at a height of 25 metres when the engine suddenly cut out and the aircraft fell towards the ground. In desperation, Blériot climbed out of his seat and threw himself towards the tail. The aircraft pulled out of the dive, and landed in a more or less horizontal position. Fortunately, his only injuries were some minor cuts to his face.

In February 1908, a British newspaper announced that it was offering £500 prize money for the first person to make the flight between England and France, before the end of that year. When 1908 passed with no serious attempt to make the flight across the Channel, the prize money was doubled to £1000 and the offer extended to the end of 1909.

On 25 July 1909, Blériot decided to make his attempt. It was one of the windiest periods of the summer, and the previous day the weather had been particularly unfavourable. Blériot got up at half-past two in the morning and took a short drive in his motor car. That was when he noticed the possibility of one brief moment of better weather between the storms. He quickly prepared his flying machine and carried out a practice flight around Calais. Everything was working well with his aircraft and he immediately flew off and headed towards England.

The distance of the flight was about 45 kilometres, his speed was around 70 kilometres an hour and he flew at an altitude of 45 to 90 metres. He did not take a compass for direction, but followed the ship *Escopette*, which guided him towards Dover. During the flight the visibility deteriorated and Blériot later said, "For more than ten minutes I was alone and lost and couldn't see anything on the horizon." Fortunately, the clouds lifted and he was able to land his aircraft near Dover Castle, on the cliffs. The actual contact with land was very hard. In fact, not only was the aircraft's propeller broken, but part of the framework which carried the engine was also damaged. However, these damages were small compared to the success of the flight. Blériot had crossed the Channel, had won the £1000 prize and had survived uninjured.

After his success, Blériot began his own aviation company and produced 900 aircraft in the next five years. In 1927, when Charles Lindbergh became the first person to fly across the Atlantic Ocean from the USA to France, Louis Blériot was there to meet him at the airfield. They were surely two of the bravest men that ever flew an aircraft and they pioneered an industry that very soon, in the 1930s, started to develop the modern-day jet engines that we all know today.

(a) What was the nationality of the first person to fly across the Channel?

.... [1]

(b) When did Blĕriot first become keen on flying?

.... [1]

(c) Why was the World Fair exhibition important for Blériot?

.... [1]

(d) How did Blériot try to prevent his aircraft crashing? Give **two** details.

.... [2]

(e) Why was the prize money increased?

.... [1]

(f) How was the weather a problem for Blériot?

.... [1]

(g) What did Blériot observe during his car ride?

.... [1]

(h) How did Blériot manage to steer a straight course to England?

.... [1]

(i) Which years were especially significant in aviation history and why were they important? Give **four** details.

....

....

....

.... [4]

[Total: 13]

Study tips

It is tempting to write long answers, but complete sentences are not usually necessary. Often, two or three words are enough to convey the key information. Sometimes, students write more than they need to for these types of question. For example, in question (b) which of these two answers do you think is better?

1) he had become very interested in flying aircraft while he was at school
2) while he was at school

 Self-assessment

Now check your answers by looking at the end of the book. When you mark your own work for this question, note that the words underlined in the answer grid *must* be in your answer to gain a mark. You can overlook some spelling and grammar mistakes unless you think that they are so wrong that any person reading your answer would not understand it.

EXERCISE 2 • Reading	
Type of task:	This is a reading exercise. You will read a text of approximately 650 words which will test all your reading skills. The task is a matching task: you will match statements to the person who has made the statement. It is likely that four different people will give accounts of their views on the same topic – but each person will present different views. Each person is likely to have written around 160 words, and the format will be diaries, blog entries or similar short pieces with a semi-formal register.
You will be assessed on:	• identifying and retrieving facts and details • recognising and selecting relevant information • understanding what is implied in the text, such as the writer's feelings or opinions
Number of questions and marks:	There are 10 short statements which you assign to one of four people. Each is worth 1 mark. Total of 10 marks

 Preparing for this type of question

A key skill for success for this question is to be able to see the differences in the detail and in the opinions that people have about the same topic. For example, the same four people who all say they like the movies may like four very different types of films. One may like going to see comedies, another may prefer science fiction, the third person might be a fan of romance films and the last person may like to go and see fantasy films. They each like films but they have different interests. If all four people were to take part in a discussion about the movies they would be able to share and compare details about their preferred genres.

You can match the statements in any order you like, but it might be best to start with the ones you are very sure about, and then spend time scanning the text for the ones you are not so sure about. This exercise requires you to read through the full text so that you can get a sense of how each person approaches the topic. Once you have got the gist of all four, you can then use your scanning skills to look for the specific information required.

 **Exercise 2**

Read the article about four people (**A-D**) who go regularly to the cinema. Then answer Question **10 (a)-(j)**.

GOING TO THE MOVIES

Four people share their thoughts on films and the cinema.

A I've been going to the movies since I was about ten years old, when my mother and father used to take me every week. Now that I am 16 years old, I go on my own of course, or with my friends. What I like about going to the cinema is that it gets me out of the house, and gives me the chance to meet up with my friends on a regular basis. If we didn't have our weekly trip to the local cinema, I think we'd all just stay in our houses on our own and probably play games on our consoles. We have built up a strong friendship group now, based on the movies. Although our trips don't exactly keep us very fit, they do give us more exercise than just staying in our rooms. In fact, last week, it was raining so heavily that we ended up running to the cinema, so we got as much exercise as if we'd gone to the local athletics track.

B I am trying to become an actor, so my trips to the cinema are partly about watching the actors on screen and learning how they go about their work. When I was very young, about 8 years old, I was given the main role in a play at my school. I remember that I enjoyed it. I was a little intimidated but I responded very well to my nerves and it made me focus more on giving a better performance. When I was a teenager I became fascinated with films and how acting in a film might be different to being on stage in a play, so I carried out some research about acting. I also explored acting as a possible career for myself. And here I am now, a student of film at university in London. The great thing is that we get to make short films and we get to act in them.

C I think that films are a vital part of modern life. Almost everyone surely goes to see a film at the cinema every now and again. But why do they go? Well, for some it is just a break from the routine of daily life and their mundane work. For others, it is a way to relax for a couple of hours with a drink and a bag of popcorn. Others might go because they get hooked on a specific genre and can't bear to miss the latest science fiction movie. Films often show us about our society and how we live, so I can come out of the cinema having watched a movie that has made me feel in touch with the rest of humanity. I know that sounds like a powerful thing but it's true – films are made by people for people. For us all to learn from, to share emotions, and to relate to some of the highs and lows that people go through in life.

D I only go to see old movies. Some of them are now over 80 years old and are in black and white of course, but also, have no sound. These are called *silent movies*. I stopped watching modern films many years ago… I prefer the style and sophistication of the older genres, such as *film noir*, which were detective stories made into films in the 1950s. Most of these films were American. I particularly like the films made between 1945 and 1970. You might be thinking where I could go to watch such old movies? Well, there are lots of specialist cinemas around the country now, so I do have to travel, but it's worth the journey to sit in a traditional cinema and enjoy these classic films as movie-goers of 50 years ago would have done. And I'm never alone; there's quite a community of people like me, seeking out the old films. I'm a member now of two classic movies' clubs.

The questions below are about the people (A–D) who write about films.
For each question write the correct letter A, B, C or D on the line.
Which person …

(a) sees going to the movies as a way of maintaining friends? .... [1]

(b) made a good job of an early role on stage? .... [1]

(c) thinks that some people can get addicted to films? .... [1]

(d) believes that going to the movies can break the daily routine? .... [1]

(e) has considered a career in the movie industry? .... [1]

(f) doesn't mind travelling a long way to see a film? .... [1]

(g) did some exercise one day because of a film? .... [1]

(h) is studying films? .... [1]

(i) prefers films made by a different generation? .... [1]

(j) thinks that working on a stage could be very different? .... [1]

[Total: 10]

Self-assessment

9-10 marks suggests that you are very good at scanning and synthesising skills. Synthesising means being able to find a common element from a range of sources. You have understood the approach needed for this type of exercise and you can locate specific detail, and infer attitudes and opinions of people.

7-8 marks suggests that you have competent and sound comprehension skills. You have probably just made a couple if minor errors and this is nothing to worry about as you will improve with more practice.

5-6 marks shows partial understanding, but an acceptable overall mark. More practice is likely to help you refine these skills of synthesising and zooming in on the specific detail needed.

1-4 marks means that you have struggled to identify what some of the people mean by what they say or by how they say it. You would benefit by looking again at each of the statements now that you know the answers to work out where you went wrong. Advice from a teacher, friend or parent might be useful. You also probably need more time to become familiar with semi-formal language in this register, such as diaries, blogs, letters to magazines. We encourage you to practise reading a range of this style of writing.

EXERCISE 3 • Note-taking	
Type of task:	This is a note-taking exercise. You will read an article and write brief notes related to information in it. You will need to convey all key words and ideas in your answer, but will not need to write in full sentences.
You will be assessed on:	• identifying and retrieving facts and relevant information • recognising opinions and attitudes and the connections between related ideas
Number of questions and marks:	The Extended paper asks for nine notes. Each note is worth 1 mark. <div align="right">Total of 9 marks</div>

 Preparing for the question

Your answers have to be written on a note-taking form under two or three headings which are given to you. Start by looking at these headings so that you have an idea what specific information you are looking for in the reading text.

When you find a relevant detail in the text, transfer it to the form and make your answer as short as possible. You should write a note and not a full sentence, but you must make sure that key words are included in your answer – don't make it so brief that you leave out important details.

 Study tips

Sometimes, students write too much for each answer. Which of these two answers do you think is best?

1) They have to make sure that the central area of the site is clean and tidy

2) clean and tidy central area

If you think the second answer, then you are right because the key details are all conveyed very clearly without the full sentence. How do you know if you are writing too much? Here is a good tip. If you can't fit your answer on one line without going into the margin, then you should think about what detail you can leave out because it may well be unimportant.

What is wrong with the following answer?

• collect wood and light fires

If you wrote this then you would only get 1 mark because you have not separated the two different ideas. To get 2 marks you need to write each answer on different lines.

 Self-assessment

When you self-assess this question, if there are two answers on a line you only mark the first answer.

You can't give yourself 2 marks if two answers repeat the same idea even though they are on separate lines and you use different words.

What about spelling and grammar? Incorrect spelling and grammar do not always mean that the answer is wrong. You should look and see how serious the mistake is and decide if the answer is still clear. Now check your answers by looking at the back of the book.

Exercise 3

Read the article about a different way of camping, and then complete the notes.

A GREAT COMBINATION: BOOKS AND AN OUTDOOR LIFE

We arrive at the campsite and the tents, formed in a large circle, are the first sign of life that we have seen for miles. In the middle of this area is a glowing camp fire. The campers are a group of about 50 teenagers on an adventure weekend in the countryside, with the combined theme of outdoor survival and studying books and literature. It is part of a growing popular trend to engage the interest of young people with books by turning books into real-life adventures and connecting teenagers with nature in the process.

The camps are based on popular books and the teenagers live and sleep like the heroes and heroines of the stories. The idea of the organisers is to introduce literature in a new way and the main emphasis is in allowing the young people to find their own adventures. The organisers believe that independent thought and behaviour are essential ingredients of growing up, but that they are lacking in many young people's lives. In their normal day, many teenagers go from lesson to lesson, from club to club, but they are not allowed to have just a little bit of freedom.

A 15-year-old girl says "We can do whatever we want here, that is the best thing about being at the camp. We are responsible for ourselves, no-one tells us what to do, the organisers trust us." There are, of course, some adults keeping a watchful eye but on the whole the young people can organise their own life. They are free to roam the forest, light fires, get really dirty and go to bed late. There is a toilet block for washing, but it seems likely that many of the campers will not have brushed their teeth or even washed their face during their week-long stay. There are, however, no showers. While mornings are free time, the afternoons consist of reading and studying books as well as activities, led by an instructor.

An important part of the philosophy is that children have to show due care and respect for others. Every day, towards the end of the afternoon, all the campers have to head into the forest to collect wood and they all have a duty to light the fires for cooking. The evening meal is followed by singing, storytelling, hot chocolate and a night time version of hide-and-seek in the forest. Before they finally go to bed in their tents, they all have to make sure that the central area of the site is clean and tidy. As is often the case with camping, it rains hard throughout most of the night and into the next morning, but the teenagers' spirits are not dampened.

Bringing literature to life in the great outdoors is the perfect way to get young people involved. The organisers believe that books are not just about a solitary experience, reading alone in your bedroom. This activity week shows to young readers that there is so much more to literature than punctuation and spelling. It is true that writing has to have these things, but to get a young person really passionate about reading you first need to start on a level which involves adventure and imagination.

You have been asked to give a talk to your school's book club about the camp. Prepare some notes to use as the basis of your talk.

Make your notes under each heading.

Description of the camp

- ....

- ....

- ....

Philosophy of the organisers

- ....

- ....

- ....

- ....

Daily tasks of the teenagers in the camp

- ....

- ....

[Total: 9]

EXERCISE 4 • Summary	
Type of task:	This is a summary writing exercise. You will read an article and write a summary about an aspect or aspects of it. You will need to convey as many relevant details as possible within a limit of either 80 or 120 words.
You will be assessed on:	• identifying and retrieving relevant information and ideas • communicating in writing clearly, accurately and appropriately • using and controlling grammatical structures including punctuation and spelling
Number of questions and marks:	For the Extended level paper, reading and writing skills are assessed: 8 marks for reading and 8 marks for writing. The checklist on page 19 will help you understand how these marks are awarded. Total of 16 marks

 Preparing for the question

Read the question carefully to make sure that you only write about the required information and ignore all the irrelevant details in the text. The text is about four times longer than your summary, so there will be many details that you do not need to include. Firstly, you should try to find the content points and make a note of them.

When you write your summary, try to change the words in the text and use your own expressions. Be careful: your wording must exactly convey the original idea and meaning in the text.

 Study tips

It is a good idea to use linking words to connect your content points, rather than just list them. Which of these styles do you think is better?

1) Firstly, robots can help us when we are travelling, especially when we want to buy automated tickets. In addition, they are likely to reduce traffic accidents as well as making our journeys safer.

Or:

2) Robots help to buy automated tickets. They reduce traffic accidents. They can make our journeys safer.

Both the above examples have the correct content, but the first answer would receive more marks for language because it has a better style and is more pleasant to read.

Exercise 4

Read the following article about robots and their role in the future. Write a summary about the main areas where robots will be able to help us in the future.

Your summary should be about 100 words long (and no more than 120 words long).

You should use your own words as far as possible.

You will receive up to 8 marks for the content of your summary, and up to 8 marks for the style and accuracy of your language.

MACHINES THAT RULE THE WORLD

Technology is transforming our lives. Indeed, digital technology is advancing so fast that computers could soon solve every problem that we face.

In future, a single digital ticket will transport us across land, sea and air by means of driverless private taxis and automated trains, buses and other public transport systems. It is predicted that commuting to work in an automated vehicle will be common in 2025. These automated vehicles will have the benefit of being able to cut the amount of transport accidents and to reduce the number of private cars.

Social networks, smartphone apps and countless inter-connected services are helping machines to learn about us as humans so quickly that by 2025 we will be able to talk to artificially intelligent 'personal assistants' as if they were human beings. This evolution is being led by a process known as 'machine learning' whereby a computer is fed huge amounts of data from which it is able to draw its own meanings. Machine learning will be crucial for advances in robotics for hospitals, home care and transport over the next decade.

In health care, for example, medical supplies will be delivered by a drone as a first response to emergencies in remote areas. In hospitals, robot assistants will increase the surgeon's ability to carry out precision operations. Robot-controlled medical tools will operate on delicate body tissue with a light touch beyond the capability of a human. Robots that can be swallowed will perform precision operations inside patients, finding their way to the right part of the body and releasing drugs or carrying out simple surgery. Automated porters will transport patients between wards and deliver their meals, and robot cleaners will work to ensure clean medical facilities and to combat infection.

As the world population becomes older, companion robots for the elderly will become normal. They will alert a family member if an elderly relative has an accident or is acting strangely.

There will be limits to the progress of this development, however. The idea of a 'general duty' robot will not come for a long time, but robots will begin to appear where they have a clearly defined role. That explains why there are already so many robots on car production lines, for example. Throughout history, we have developed extraordinary capabilities as humans, but it has taken us centuries to reach our present stage of evolution. The idea of a humanoid robot has been constantly promoted in science fiction books, films and articles, but for the moment it is just that… fiction and not fact.

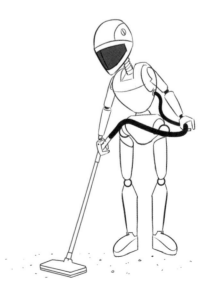

....

....

....

....

....

....

....

....

....

....

....

....

....

....

....

....

....

....

....

[Total: 16]

Self-assessment

Checklist for marking use of language in summary writing

Use the guidelines below to arrive at a mark out of 8 for the **language** that you used in this exercise.

When I finished my written piece I felt...	Yes	No	If yes, ...
I was confident with my writing and tried very hard to change words and expressions in the text and use my own without making any mistakes. I also concentrated on making the details flow nicely with linking words.			Give yourself 7 or 8 marks.
I made some effort to change words here and there. I thought that my language was correct most of the time.			Give yourself 5 or 6 marks.
I was less confident about changing too many words from the original text and tended to stay with safer, simpler language so that I didn't make mistakes.			Give yourself 3 or 4 marks.
I didn't try to change any words and just simply copied the original. I wasn't able to include any linking words and I felt that I made mistakes which would make it hard for the reader to understand what I was trying to say.			Give yourself 2 marks.
I struggled with this exercise and could only copy some detail. I am not sure if the detail was correct or not, and my language had lots of mistakes.			Give yourself 1 mark.

As well as language marks, your summary may be awarded marks for each correct **content** detail that you convey. These details are listed in the mark scheme at the back of the book.

You do not have to use the same words as in the mark scheme – in fact it is better if you use your own expressions – but you do have to convey the key details of each point.

How about practising to see if you can change the wording of the content points on the mark scheme? There are eight points, so try and use your own words to convey each idea, but make sure that you do not lose the precise meaning of each point.

For example, Medical supply deliveries could be changed to transporting drugs and equipment to hospitals.

Also, companion robots for the elderly could become robots that keep older people company.

Can you do the same thing with the other content points?

EXERCISE 5 • Writing	
Type of task:	This is a writing exercise. You will need to write a piece, such as an email or a letter to a friend or family member. Your style of writing or register should be informal.
You will be assessed on:	• writing and developing original ideas and feelings effectively • communicating with accurate grammar, punctuation and style
Number of questions and marks:	There is just one main task, but there are three bullet points to consider. You must write something for all three bullet points. <div align="right">Total of 16 marks</div>

 Preparing for the question

Before you start, think about the person you are writing to and what you need to include. It is always a good idea to write a plan, making sure that you are addressing all the bullet points. Look carefully at the wording of the bullet points, such as *explain*, *describe* and *say* and think about what you are expected to do. You should plan to write a paragraph for each bullet point and don't forget to include a brief introduction and conclusion.

When you choose your words and expressions, think about the person who is receiving the email or letter. They would like to be entertained, so choose vocabulary that is out of the ordinary. For example, how about *joyful* instead of *happy* or *gigantic* instead of *very big*? Try to use rhetorical questions, such as *Don't you think that was a good idea?* This adds variety to your writing, connects personally with the reader and gives the piece much more life.

 Study tips

Here is an example response:

We visited the Modern Science museum in Delhi. We went there because it was an extension of our science curriculum. I liked the interactive engineering displays. The visit will help me see that science can be applied and put into action.

This is an interesting response because it contains some useful and relevant ideas, but it has combined all three bullet points into one paragraph. It is much better to take each idea and develop it into its own paragraph. For example, the student could have said more about the nature of the interactivity of the engineering displays. Therefore, it is best not to mix up the separate ideas in the three bullet points.

Exercise 5

Your school class recently visited a museum as part of your science course.

Write an email to a friend about this experience.

In your email you should:

- explain which museum you visited and why;
- describe the most interesting part of the museum;
- say how this visit will help you with your science studies.

Your email should be between 150 and 200 words long. Do not write an address.

The pictures above may give you some ideas, and you should try to use some ideas of your own.

You will receive up to 8 marks for the content of your email, and up to 8 marks for the style and accuracy of your language.

....

....

....

....

....

....

....

....

....

....

....

....

....

....

....

....

....

....

....

....

....

[Total: 16]

Self-assessment

Two criteria are used to mark this exercise: **content** and **language**, both of which have a maximum mark of 8.

We have converted these into easy-to-use checklists for you.

When I finished my written piece I felt...	Yes	No	If yes, ...
Content			
I developed my ideas very well, writing lots of extra detail. I made sure that I referred to the reader all the time, with a correct formal or informal style. I thought that the reader would find my writing very enjoyable.			Give yourself 8 marks.
I completed all the parts of the task and added some extra ideas and detail. I remembered who I was writing for and wrote in a style that was appropriate.			Give yourself 6 or 7 marks.
My style of writing was OK and I made sure that my piece was always about the subject, but I was not able to add much extra detail.			Give yourself 5 marks.
I wasn't sure that I was successful in keeping to the topic all the time. I didn't have too many ideas and felt that I wrote some things which were not really relevant.			Give yourself 4 marks.
I didn't really think about who was going to read the piece and wrote in the wrong style. I also felt that I was short of ideas and repeated myself at times.			Give yourself 2 or 3 marks.
Language			
I was confident with my writing and used a wide range of very accurate language and even managed to include some good idioms. I made sure that my verb tenses were all correct. All in all, I thought that I made very few errors.			Give yourself 8 marks.
I tried to use some more unusual words and expressions and think that I was generally accurate with them. I remembered to use paragraphs to divide the different ideas that I had.			Give yourself 6 or 7 marks.
I tended to stay with safer, simpler language so that I didn't make mistakes.			Give yourself 4 or 5 marks.
I found the writing hard, made too many mistakes and maybe the person reading my piece would have had problems at times trying to understand it.			Give yourself 2 or 3 marks.

Now add up your marks from the two checklists, to arrive at a mark out of 16.

If your total mark is in the range:

- 14–16: you are doing really well
- 10–13: this is fine, but more practice is likely to help you a lot
- 7–9: it's a safe and secure performance
- 0–6: you are struggling a little and you should practise as much as you can, developing more ideas and working hard to get your verb tenses correct. Start with short paragraphs one at a time and gradually develop them.

EXERCISE 6 • Writing	
Type of task:	This is a writing exercise. You will need to write a piece, such as an article for a school magazine or a letter to a newspaper. Your style of writing or register should be formal and you should try to persuade the reader of your opinions.
You will be assessed on:	• writing and developing original ideas, feelings and opinions effectively • communicating with accurate grammar, punctuation and style
Number of questions and marks:	There is just one main task, but there are two brief prompts to consider. You may use the ideas in these prompts and develop them, or think of your own ideas. <div align="right">Total of 16 marks</div>

 Preparing for the question

Think about the purpose of the piece before you start and what you need to include. It is always a good idea to write a plan, with separate, different ideas so that you don't repeat the same idea. Look carefully at the wording of the question and think about whether you are 'for' or 'against' the argument, or prefer to give a balanced view for both sides. It does not matter which approach you choose, but your writing must be convincing and persuasive. Plan to write at least two paragraphs to express your views and don't forget to include a brief introduction and conclusion.

When you choose your words and expressions, think about the person who is receiving the article or letter. They want to be convinced by your views, so choose vocabulary that is strong and out of the ordinary. For example, you could use expressions like *there is absolutely no doubt in my mind…* or *I am totally convinced that….* These add variety to your writing and persuade the reader that you are serious about the issues.

 Study tips

Read the question on page 25, then look at these two extracts taken from the middle sections of essays, written by two students. Which one do you think is better? Which is the most effective?

Student 1:

So I think that there are two sides to this issue. Yes, of course, we should use money and resources to improve people's lives on Earth, but it is not as simple as that. We also need to try to see what is out there in space. We may find friendly species, keen to help us, or we may find a planet like ours to move to when our planet gets too full…

Student 2:

It's clear to me, therefore, that we should not waste money on space travel at the moment as we have too many problems on Earth with millions of people in poverty, and struggling to live decent lives. What we may find in space in 100 years will not help them now, and it is cruel to sacrifice their lives for our desire to seek new frontiers. I believe that we should venture into space when we have solved all of our problems on earth…

As you can see they are both effective. Student 2 takes a stronger view and prefers to agree and align with the second quote, which is fine. As long as you support your view with a strong argument and examples. Student 1 prefers a more balanced response, looking at pros and cons and this is fine also.

Exercise 6

Some people think that we should not spend huge amounts of money on space research when it could be better spent on helping people on this planet.

Here are two comments about this idea:

"Space research may help us discover new worlds and other civilisations."

"So many people need help to improve their life here on Earth."

Write a letter to your local newspaper giving your views.

Your letter should be between 150 and 200 words long.

The comments above may give you some ideas, and you should try to use some ideas of your own.

You will receive up to 10 marks for the content of your letter, and up to 9 marks for the style and accuracy of your language.

....

....

....

....

....

....

....

....

....

....

....

....

....

[Total: 16]

Self-assessment

Two criteria are used to mark this exercise: **content** and **language**, both of which have a maximum mark of 8.

We have converted these into easy-to-use checklists for you.

When I finished my written piece I felt...	Yes	No	If yes, ...
Content			
I developed my ideas very well, writing lots of extra detail. I made sure that I referred to the reader all the time, with a correct formal or informal style. I thought that the reader would find my writing very enjoyable.			Give yourself 8 marks.
I completed all the parts of the task and added some extra ideas and detail. I remembered who I was writing for and wrote in a style that was appropriate.			Give yourself 6 or 7 marks.
My style of writing was OK and I made sure that my piece was always about the subject, but I was not able to add much extra detail.			Give yourself 5 marks.
I wasn't sure that I was successful in keeping to the topic all the time. I didn't have too many ideas and felt that I wrote some things which were not really relevant.			Give yourself 4 marks.
I didn't really think about who was going to read the piece and wrote in the wrong style. I also felt that I was short of ideas and repeated myself at times.			Give yourself 2 or 3 marks.
Language			
I was confident with my writing and used a wide range of very accurate language and even managed to include some good idioms. I made sure that my verb tenses were all correct. All in all, I thought that I made very few errors.			Give yourself 8 marks.
I tried to use some more unusual words and expressions and think that I was generally accurate with them. I remembered to use paragraphs to divide the different ideas that I had.			Give yourself 6 or 7 marks.
I tended to stay with safer, simpler language so that I didn't make mistakes.			Give yourself 4 or 5 marks.
I found the writing hard, made too many mistakes and maybe the person reading my piece would have had problems at times trying to understand it.			Give yourself 2 or 3 marks.

Now add up your marks from the two checklists to arrive at a mark out of 16.

If your total mark is in the range:

- 14–16: you are doing really well
- 10–13: this is fine, but more practice is likely to help you a lot
- 7–9: it's a safe and secure performance
- 0–6: you are struggling a little and you should practise as much as you can, developing more ideas and working hard to get your verb tenses correct. Start with short paragraphs one at a time and gradually develop them.

Paper 2 Listening

Overview of the questions

When you work through this practice examination paper you will be able to give yourself some marks for each question. You can add up your marks to arrive at a total for your listening skills. You should arrive at a total mark out of 40.

	Marks
Exercise 1	8
Exercise 2	8
Exercise 3	6
Exercise 4	8
Exercise 5 part a	5
Exercise 5 part b	5
Total marks	**40**

Now use the table below to see how well you have done.

Mark	Comment
33 marks and over	Excellent and things are looking great for a top grade in your examination.
27 to 32 marks	Good, you should be heading for a solid performance and a good grade in your exam.
23 to 26 marks	You can be happy with this score, but there are clearly some areas you need to review where you could improve and pick up more marks. However, you are heading for a satisfactory grade.
16 to 22 marks	There are clearly some weak or problem areas where you are losing marks, but don't panic. This is practice and you probably need more practice. We think it would be useful to get some advice and guidance from a teacher, parent or friend, so that you can see where you need to improve.

EXERCISE 1	
Type of task:	There are four short extracts. Each of the four has a different theme. Announcements or brief dialogues (formal or informal) are often used. The questions require short answers, no longer than three words each.
You will be assessed on:	• identifying and retrieving facts and details
Number of questions and marks:	There are four questions, but each one is split into two separate parts. Each question is worth 2 marks. Total of 8 marks

 Preparing for the question

Each of the four questions operates using the same pattern: the first part (a) is linked to the first main idea, and then the second part (b) follows up on this, usually with a more specific detail. For all eight items you are only listening to recall information.

For example, read the following statement by a newsreader. Can you find the main idea, and then the second idea?

> "Tonight we look in depth at a new development in treating heart disease. A new test that not only measures the disease in the arteries, but also uses a patient's DNA profile to state when the surgery should take place."

A new way of treating heart disease is the main idea, and the supporting idea then states *when treatment should take place*. Try to predict what these secondary, supportive ideas might be.

 Study tips

Read the questions on page 29, then consider these study tips. Remember that you are only allowed to write *up to three words*, so do you think this student's response is acceptable for Question 1?

1a) carry general public passengers

No, it isn't because it uses four words. Even though it is the correct answer, the student would not get the mark as he or she has not followed the instruction.

Also, what if a student provided this for Question 2a?

2a) eighteen hundred and twenty nine

Well, that's five words so no, the mark would be lost. Had the student written *eighteen twenty nine* that would be acceptable. However, it is better to write numbers in *numerical* formats (i.e. 1829).

Now, consider this answer for Question 4a:

4a) Ski Run 3

Would you allow that? It wouldn't be allowed as it doesn't answer the question, which asks for a *type* of game. The name of the game isn't a type.

🔊 Exercise 1

You will hear four short recordings. Answer each question on the line provided. Write no more than **three** words for each answer.

You can play the recording twice.

1　(a) At 50 000 feet what will this aircraft do that none has done before?

....[1]

(b) How long will the journey be from London to New York?

....[1]

2　(a) When was the steam train designed?

....[1]

(b) From where does the modern craft get its power source?

....[1]

3　(a) Which doctor's appointment does George prefer?

....[1]

(b) If George's eye problem is not connected to his neck problem, what will he have to do?

....[1]

4　(a) What type of video game is the girl looking for?

....[1]

(b) What is the restriction placed on the game?

....[1]

[Total: 8]

Self-assessment

Now check your answers using the mark scheme at the back of the book. When you mark your own work for these four questions, don't worry too much about accurate grammar. For example, the following response for Question 1(a) would be allowed:

• carrying passengers

Even though the verb tense is not what is expected, the main idea is there and the detail is correct. However, if you had written carrying passenging you would not get a mark because your answer makes less sense and the meaning becomes blurred. Therefore, make sure you get the right piece of information and if your grammar doesn't change the meaning, the occasional slip will not lose you the mark.

It is important to retrieve the detail accurately. For example, in the second part of Question 1 you are asked about the length of the journey to New York, but if you have put four hours this is not accurate as the flight time is *under* four hours, which is a different length of time. You do need to be 100% accurate and this may involve using all three words available to you.

EXERCISE 2	
Type of task:	This is a semi-formal talk and you will be asked to fill in a notepad using one or two words only.
You will be assessed on:	• identifying and retrieving facts and details • understanding and selecting relevant information
Number of questions and marks:	There will be eight notes for you to fill in, each worth 1 mark. Some of the notes are provided, so you only need to write in the empty gap to complete the other, remaining notes. Total of 8 marks

 Preparing for the question

Listening for specific information is the key skill here. There are two levels of this: simply locating a detail, but also being able to select a relevant detail from some options. Here is how it works with two made-up examples:

- The space station is 85 000 kilometres from Earth (simple fact).
- The best time to visit is in winter because the atmosphere is clearer (selecting the relevant detail).

Your practice exam question features both of these types of listening skill.

Exercise 2

5 You will hear a talk about an astronaut's experience of living and working on a space station. Listen to the talk and complete the notes below. Write **one** or **two** words or a **number** in each gap.

You can play the talk twice.

LIVING ON A SPACE STATION

Scientists and engineers are collaborating to develop space tourism.

Equipment needed for travel to the station

A pressurised ....

Which has a .... with a means of communication

Special boots heavy enough to keep you from floating away

Some issues with living in space

Many of the original problems have been solved

With little exercise bones lose ....

The wasting away of .... can be a problem

Not experiencing a simulator means some people may get ....

Food preparation and eating meals

A meal tray is used to position the various different foods in containers

Without the tray food could ....

In addition to forks, knives and spoon, ... are needed

Sleeping arrangements

No space for separate cabins

The bunks are .... to the walls

Holiday features

Fans, blankets, sheets and pillows

A space walk, but not further than ....

[Total: 8]

Study tips

Remember that you are only allowed to write one or two words in a gap, so do you think this response is acceptable in this gap?

with little exercise bones lose a lot of minerals

No, it isn't acceptable as *four* words have been used. Even though the answer is basically correct, this is a test of precise listening skills and *a lot of* was not mentioned in the talk, so additional words and an additional idea has been added.

 Self-assessment

Now check your answers using the mark scheme at the back of the book. When you mark your own work for this question, there are three answers which may be interesting:

If you wrote pair scissors rather than just *scissors*, this would be acceptable as you are allowed two words and the meaning of what you are saying is clear.

If you wrote fixed to the walls rather than *attached*, which was the word the astronaut used, then this would be acceptable as it is a synonym and means the same thing.

If you wrote ten metres then this is acceptable as writing numbers in letters works here as there are still only two words. However, if the answer was *2400* and you wrote two thousand and four hundred you would not get a mark.

EXERCISE 3	
Type of task:	There will be some short, informal monologues and you will try to match each speaker to the appropriate opinion that is expressed in the monologue.
You will be assessed on:	<ul><li>recognising and understanding ideas, opinions and attitudes</li><li>recognising the connections between related ideas</li><li>understanding what is implied but not actually stated, e.g. gist, relationships between speakers, speaker's purpose, speaker's intention</li><li>working out a speaker's feelings, situation or place</li></ul>
Number of questions and marks:	There are six speakers and seven opinions given as monologues. One of the opinions is extra and is not used. There is 1 mark for each of the six correct matches. Total of 6 marks

 Preparing for the question

This question is focused on recognising opinions. All of the speakers you hear will have similar and different opinions about a single topic or theme. In this practice question, the theme is how modern forms of social media communication are affecting people's lives. You will hear both the positive and the negative effects, but you might also hear people saying that the effects are neutral and need to be observed.

The statements on the exam paper will be shortened versions – or summaries – of what each speaker says, but some of the words will have been changed from what you hear in the recording. This is to also test your understanding of the gist (general idea) of what each of them is saying.

Remember that some of the opinions are similar, but also have a clear difference. Listen carefully for these differences as this is likely to feature on the exam paper.

An example is two people talking about nuclear power. One person says she knows we need to use it as a form of energy, but is *cautious*. The other person also appreciates we need to use it, but is *worried*. *Cautious* and *worried* are not the same opinion. Therefore, recognising what is implied, or suggested by words indicating shades of difference, is an important skill to develop to do well on Exercise 3, and also in all of your English exams!

🔊 Exercise 3

6   You will hear six people talking about modern forms of communication. For each of Speakers 1 to 6, choose from the list, **A** to **G**, which opinion each speaker expresses. Write the letter in the box. Use each letter only once. There is one extra letter which you do not need to use.

Speaker 1   ____

Speaker 2   ____

Speaker 3   ____

Speaker 4   ____

Speaker 5   ____

Speaker 6   ____

A   I think that younger people are more affected by the growth in digital communication than older people, even to the point of not eating properly.

B   The type of food eaten is the main thing. Eating the wrong food at the wrong time of day makes it harder to multi-task.

C   I don't think the problem is age-related at all. I think it's much more to do with having too many options open to us.

D   I think we should spend the same amount of time using the technology, but take the right kind of breaks during the day.

E   I think it's a feature of 21st century life that people depend on social media for their social life, but also for their careers.

F   I feel that, at my stage of life, technology is over-taking me and I need things to be more straightforward.

G   I don't think the balance is about time spent using or not using the technology. It's about using the technology to work for you and taking the chance to learn something new!

[Total: 6]

Self-assessment

Now check your answer using the mark scheme at the back of the book. It might be helpful to consider the following points:

Speaker 1 may agree with statements A, D, E and G, but is not likely to have said C as that statement is clear that the problem is not age-related.

Speaker 2 would not agree with A and hasn't mentioned the idea in B at all, so we don't know the view held on food. Also, D, E and G are areas that have not been mentioned in the monologue (i.e. life/work balance, and using social media for work). Statement F is interesting as we don't know the age of the speaker and there is reference to the ages of people affected. However, it is unlikely that this speaker would fully agree with F, even though the idea of being overloaded is there, as the speaker isn't suggesting a simple or straightforward solution or using less technology.

Speaker 3 would not agree with C as there is a clear view on an age-related fact. Statements D, E, F and G are too broad in their coverage, while Speaker 3 talks only about 18–24 year olds and about them spending too long using smart technology in the mornings, which results in missing breakfast. Statement B is interesting as it mentions food, but with the focus on the type of food and not the particular meal of the day.

Speaker 4 focuses on the connection between digital communication tools and work/careers. Therefore, you would look for a statement which mentions work and/or careers. This is a case where you can use scanning skills – and you can see that statement G mentions work but focuses on multi-tasking, and statement D implies taking a break from work – but neither statement is as clear about the impact on careers as E.

Speaker 5, for this only statements D and G can be considered, and as G mentions a work/life balance, statement D is the most accurate as it focuses on balance in general.

Speaker 6 promotes multi-tasking and developing a wider range of skills as more devices are engaged with, so the only statement that fits is G. If you chose statement E, you were not too far away, though a similar idea can be inferred, but statement G covers all of the points made in the recording.

As you can see, this is an exercise in deciding which statement fits best and is the most accurate from the list of seven provided. Some statements will usually just not apply as they will present very different or opposite opinions and you can look for these first and disregard them, leaving you to focus on the ones that might work.

Another point is some of what a speaker says may well agree with a statement and you may have given yourself a mark on that basis, but *all* of what is in the statement must match what the speaker says in the recording.

EXERCISE 4	
Type of task:	You will listen to a semi-formal discussion between two speakers.
You will be assessed on:	• recognising and understanding ideas, opinions and attitudes • recognising the connections between related ideas • understanding what is implied but not actually stated, e.g. gist, relationships between speakers, speaker's purpose, speaker's intention • working out a speaker's feelings, situation or place
Number of questions and marks:	There are eight questions worth 1 mark each. They are all multiple choice questions and you will choose from three options: A, B or C. One of these is a distractor, which means it is there to purposefully lead you away from the correct answer. Total of 8 marks

 Preparing for the question

The listening skills for this question, which appears towards the end of your examination, are at a higher level than just locating specific information. Here, you are required to infer, to work out what has been implied. The questions are in multiple choice format, so you will need to think carefully about which of the three answers is the most accurate. Here's how it works:

A medical researcher, called Ivan, said in an interview that new evidence suggested that ex-athletes who exercise too much after they retire can actually do more damage to their hearts than non-athletes who exercise moderately. A question based on this statement for Exercise 4 might look like this:

a) *What is Ivan's advice to people who used to be athletes and who still exercise?*

A To exercise to their fullest potential.

B To exercise only moderately.

C To exercise, but to seek medical advice.

Did you choose B? If so, then yes, that is the most appropriate answer as the new evidence suggests that athletes are at risk if they carry on exercising a lot because their heart health is threatened. In choosing B you have worked this out based on the opinion of the researcher and the related idea of heart health to athletes.

Exercise 4

(7) You will hear a TV presenter talking to Sarah, who is a medical researcher. Listen to their conversation and look at the questions. For each question choose the correct answer, **A**, **B** or **C**, and put a tick (✓) in the appropriate box.

You can play the talk twice.

(a) How is the new fitband different to those already on the market?

    A It measures heart rate and blood pressure. ☐

    B It measures variations in a person's DNA. ☐

    C It measures one person's DNA against another person's DNA. ☐   [1]

(b) The fitband is able to

    A advise you not to exercise. ☐

    B advise you to take a day off from the gym. ☐

    C advise you that you may have an infection. ☐   [1]

(c) The research team's second phase objective is to

    A capture one year of data. ☐

    B capture five months of data. ☐

    C capture 80 people to test the new device. ☐   [1]

(d) The fitband is an improvement on current monitoring methods because

    A it carries out checks every day. ☐

    B it carries out checks on an on-going basis. ☐

    C it carries out checks using snapshots. ☐   [1]

(e) The reliability of the fitband depends on

    A getting five months' worth of data. ☐

    B getting data on a monthly basis. ☐

    C getting a set amount of data. ☐   [1]

(f) Sarah believes that the new device will help to

    A predict diabetes in a person. ☐

    B cure diabetes. ☐

    C stop a person getting diabetes. ☐ [1]

(g) How might this device be particularly advantageous for governments?

    A It can reduce disease. ☐

    B It can save them money. ☐

    C It can make the population fitter. ☐ [1]

(h) In the near future, the main problem with the data is that

    A it will be more unreliable. ☐

    B it will be more difficult to capture. ☐

    C it will need to be made secure on other devices. ☐ [1]

[Total: 8]

Self-assessment

Now check your answers using the mark scheme at the back of the book. The following advice may help you.

Question a) Answer A is not actually wrong but it doesn't show how the new device is *different*. The difference is the key word in the question. Answer C is a distractor as it covers the right content (e.g. DNA) but adds a new idea: the idea that another person's DNA is considered is not actually in the recording. It distracts you from the main evidence. Always look out for additional information which may be true or not true, but cannot be proved either way.

Question b) Multiple choice answers will usually have very similar 'stems' – these make the potential answers look alike. For this question the word *advise* is the stem. Answer B is very close, but if you listen carefully, you will hear that it's the interviewer who states this and not information from the device. Answer A is an inference because you can work out that you shouldn't exercise, but there is no evidence in the recording that the wrist band has given this advice. Therefore, be careful and make sure the answer you choose has clear evidence in the recording.

Question c) Notice how *capture* appears as the stem, but notice also that it doesn't appear in the recording. They use *produce* which in context means the same as *capture*. This is a common way to test your understanding. Also, when you have numbers, dates, times, etc. you will see them tested. Answer B is the distractor because *five months* is the time that the current users have had the device. Answer C is also inaccurate because the 80 people have already been identified. In fact, only answer A is correct because it is the only statement that relates to phase 2 of the project!

Question d) Answer C is the distractor as the snapshots refer to the current devices and methods used, so this is incorrect. Answer A also distracts: in the recording we hear *for that day* and that might be misunderstood as *every day*. Therefore, be careful with the actual listening – you are being tested on how successfully you listen to what has actually been said. It is important to recognise that *for that day* and *every day* are different things.

Question e) This is another question about hearing and understanding time, in terms of a period of time on this occasion. Listen carefully for numbers. Answer A is clearly wrong. These are the easiest multiple choice answers to mark since in the recording it is stated clearly that five months is not enough time. Also, answer B is not the right answer, but you do have to work this out from *we don't think this is the best method*. Answer C uses *certain* as synonymous with *set*.

Question f) This question is a little different because the stem is made to look similar with the length of the statements, but you need to understand the difference between *predict*, *cure* and *stop*. If you do, then answer A is straightforward, but you do need to match *predict* with *give indications of*. In this case, answer B and C are both wrong as there is no evidence of the device being able to cure or stop a disease.

Question g) This is really testing your skill in inferring, or working out what is implied. Answers A and C are distractors in that they are both correct and will help everyone, including governments. However, answer B is the *best* answer as it contains the accurate and specific detail.

Question h) It is pretty clear that answer A is wrong as the security (so reliability) of the data is safe. Answer B is interesting as it needs you to understand exactly what *capture* means. The wrist band is a capture device and it has already been established that there are no problems with this, so there is no evidence that it will become more difficult in the future. Answer C picks up on the concern when *other* devices are used, so C is the only viable response.

In conclusion, our advice is that you always consider *all* three responses in Exercise 4: there are reasons why each one is there, and if you can see the rationale for a response, you are more likely to be successful in choosing it, or avoiding it!

EXERCISE 5	
Type of task:	There are two parts to this question, Part A and Part B, but they are connected. You will hear a talk for Part A, given by one person, and in Part B, you will hear a dialogue between two people about the talk (i.e. picking up on various aspects of the talk). The task for Part A requires you to complete short notes with one or two words. The task for Part B requires you to also use only one or two words, but to complete gaps in sentences. The talk will be of a semi-formal nature, but the discussion afterwards is likely to be informal.
You will be assessed on:	• identifying and retrieving facts and details • understanding and selecting relevant information • recognising and understanding ideas, opinions and attitudes • recognising the connections between related ideas • understanding what is implied but not actually stated, e.g. gist, relationships between speakers, speaker's purpose, speaker's intention • working out a speaker's feelings, situation or place
Number of questions and marks:	In Part A there are five notes to fill in worth 1 mark each. In Part B there are five sentences to complete worth 1 mark each. <div align="right">Total of 10 marks</div>

 Preparing for the question

Part A

You are preparing for two types of question, but you are only allowed to use one or two words to provide the answers for both. Taking into account both parts of Question 8, you will be practising all of the listening skills tested in the exam. In Part A, the focus will be on the first two points in the table above, and Part B will focus on points 3 to 6.

Here's how it works: in a semi-formal talk, the main aim is usually to provide some information to the listener. In your practice exam in Unit 1, a salt mine is used as the location for the talk so you can expect some information related to the mining of salt. For example, the speaker may have said that:

> "With the <u>15 000 tonnes of salt we produce each day</u>, we can easily cope with our severe winters, and we can clear the roads <u>in a 120 mile radius</u> based on what we produce and have in stock."

The specific information provided is underlined. However, you have only one or two words to convey this information, so on the exam paper you will not be asked for all of the detail. Attention to detail is a key skill for you to develop, so that you can identify the particular information required. Therefore, Part A is focused on identifying details.

Preparing for the question

Part B

In the discussion below, try to imagine yourself being there also, having listened to the talk. What kinds of things would you have responded with, or asked your friend about? You will hear the conversation between two of the people in the audience. For example, they may have said this:

> Person 1: "Wow. They are going to use the tunnels in the mine to shoot a James Bond car chase. How exciting!"

> Person 2: "I'd love to see that. Those tunnels must be dark and eerie. Great for a spy film."

Here you can see that the register moves from semi-formal to informal conversational, and this is how Part B picks up from Part A. A key skill to learn is asking (and answering) questions based on a talk. Part B is focused on the relationship between two speakers and working out their feelings.

It is useful to note that in Part B it is a two-way dialogue, with both people sharing ideas, views and feelings (i.e. it is not like other dialogues on the exam paper where an interviewer asks questions and a subject provides the answers). It is important to be prepared to answer questions about what *both* people say in this final section of the exam.

 Study tips

Part A

Remember that you are only allowed to write one or two words as notes. Therefore, do you think the following response is acceptable?

- the mine is no longer a working coal mine

No, it isn't acceptable as three words have been used. Even though the answer is still correct, you will not get the mark if you have gone over the allowed word limit. You need to be selective and choose the best two words – or if it works, just a single word. In the case above, either *working mine* or *coal mine* would work and would be acceptable as they both communicate a solid answer. However, *working coal* would not be accepted as the meaning is in doubt – what is a *working coal*? Choose one or two words, but make sure that the meaning of the note is very clear.

Part B

In this section it is important to use the correct grammar to complete the sentence. In light of this, do you think the following would be given a mark?

- if our professor likes the idea, we can made an appointment with Mr Johansen

No, it wouldn't get a mark because the verb tense is wrong. The word *made* implies that the act has already been done and the appointment made. We need *make* here to confirm that the act will take place in the future. It is important to get your tenses and grammar correct in this section, as the sentences you create must make sense.

 **Exercise 5**

8 (a) You will hear a man called Mr Johansen giving a talk about a salt mine in Sweden and the various uses of the mine. Listen to the talk and complete the notes in part A. Write one or two words only in each gap.

You can play the talk twice.

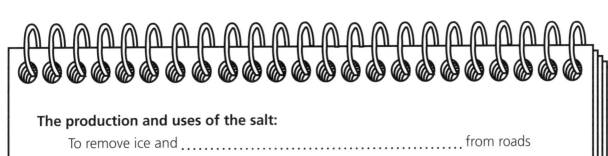

The production and uses of the salt:

To remove ice and .... from roads

On a daily basis 15 000 tonnes are mined

Half a million tonnes are stored above ground

Alternative uses for the salt mine:

A storage business

To store items which require a constant, cool temperature

Currently housing 2.8 ....

National film archives are stored in the chambers

Some geological .... are stored in the tunnels

The next James Bond film will use the tunnels for a car chase

How the salt is extracted:

Machines powered by electricity take out walls of rock salt

The rock salt is conveyed to the .... where it is crushed

25% of the rock salt is left to support the new roofs

A .... is added to stop the salt binding

An interesting fact:

The word *salary* comes from Roman soldiers who used their money to buy salt

[Total: 5]

 **Exercise 5**

8 (b) Now listen to a conversation between Renaldo and his college friend, Kristen, about their day at the salt mine. Complete the sentences in part B. Write one or two words only in each gap.

You can play the conversation twice.

A project for students at the salt mine

(a) Kristen was more interested in the .... than anything else.

(b) Renaldo said that the tunnels were .... than the local racing circuit.

(c) Renaldo suggests that their college .... could be carried out at the mine.

(d) Kristen thinks that the tunnels will contain some .... of rocks.

(e) Both students agree that some .... might also be inside the boxes.

[Total: 5]

Self-assessment

Part A

Check your answers by using the mark scheme at the back of the book. When you are marking your answers to this question the following advice may help you.

> To remove ice and snow from roads

Only one word is needed here. If you had put *clear snow* however, then this would be fine as it conveys the right idea and uses two words.

> Currently housing 2.8 million boxes

In this note, it is important to remember the quantity. 2.8 *boxes* is a very different number of boxes (it is just under 3 boxes!).

> Some geological rock samples are stored in the tunnels

You may have chosen *rocks* but this would not be allowed as it is too general; the *samples* element is important. You may have rock sample and this would be allowed as the plural isn't critical here (the meaning is the same whether singular or plural).

> The rock salt is conveyed to the surface where it is crushed

What about if you didn't know the word *surface*, but you understood the meaning of the notes in context, so you wrote *exterior.* Well, this would be allowed as exterior is a synonym for surface. However, be careful as the new word must mean the same, so *roof* would not be allowed. If you put *very top part* it wouldn't be allowed as there are three words.

> A liquid product is added to stop the salt binding

You may have put only product or even just liquid. Well, product would not be allowed as the specific detail of it being a liquid has not been given, but liquid without product works in the note to convey the key idea and so that would be allowed. If you are relaying exactly what you have heard though you should be writing liquid product!

Part B

A difference in this section is that you are given full sentences, rather than notes. Therefore, remember to ensure that what you add to the gaps helps create a full and proper sentence. Indeed the resulting sentence must flow and the words inserted must be grammatically accurate. You can still be slightly out with your spelling, but the grammar must be secure.

Here's what we mean:

a) If you had put car chasing this would be fine as your sentence is still accurate.

b) If you had used long instead of long<u>er</u> you wouldn't be allowed a mark, for two reasons: firstly, your sentence isn't grammatically accurate; but secondly, you need the comparative here to show you have understood clearly.

c) Remember that you can use two words, but to try and use only one if you can. Therefore, here you may have put based project and this would be fine. However, project is all you actually need.

d) For this sentence the answer is rare samples. You must have *rare* as this is an important adjective. If you just put samples the idea is only partially correct. The emphasis on the rarity of the rocks is important, so sometimes you *do* need to use two words.

e) This sentence is interesting as you have several options, and in each of these cases you would get a mark:

organisations' junk   crime records   court cases

Therefore, if you convey the right meaning by using different words, this is fine. If you put records on its own that wouldn't be given a mark though as more specific detail is needed.

Paper 3 Speaking

Overview

It is most likely that you will take a 15 minute speaking test towards the end of your course. This is a formal examination and you will be tested in an examination room with a teacher who is acting as an examiner. Therefore, your test will be marked initially by your teacher/examiner and then sent to an external moderator.

EXERCISE 1 • Speaking	
Type of task:	There are 10 test cards with 10 different themes. However, your examiner will choose the topic/theme and present the card to you. You are not allowed to choose your own test card. You can look at the card for a few minutes and think of what you might say and how the discussion might develop. The main part of the exam lasts for 6–9 minutes and it is during this part that you will be assessed. Before you are given the card, there is a 2–3 minute warm-up during which the examiner will help settle you down with some general conversation.
You will be assessed on:	• **Structure** The range you use and how accurately you control them. Think of this as the accuracy of your spoken language. • **Vocabulary** How precise and competent your use of words is. At the higher level, can you convey shades of meaning? At a secure level, is your vocabulary sufficient to convey your ideas clearly? • **Development** Your ability to sustain and expand upon the discussion. At the higher level, can you respond to changes of direction and can you contribute at some length? • **Fluency** This is really a measure of how clear your pronunciation and intonation is. Does your speaking flow naturally, using appropriate tone, emphasis, stressing of certain words, etc.?
Number of questions and marks:	You will be presented with a single test card which has a main theme to discuss, followed by five bullet points to help you contribute and develop the conversation. Each of the five prompts serves a different purpose and together they help build the discussion, making it more sophisticated as it progresses. The five prompts can be thought of as questions, though on the card they are given as statements. The examiner will use all five prompts. You will be awarded up to: 10 marks for structure 10 marks for vocabulary 10 marks for development and fluency Total of 30 marks

Preparing for the question

For this practice unit we will help you work through all five points on a test card, and you can listen to the recording and practise how to manage the expected flow of the discussion. Start by reading the main theme and the five prompts.

Now, look at prompt 1, and note that they start by asking for your personal experiences and your own views on the topic. In this case, you are expected to talk about the technology you use on a daily or regular basis, such as your mobile phone, your laptop, your game playing equipment, but also maybe cars, trains and airplanes you have used. You could even talk about technology around you (e.g. in shopping malls, cinemas, etc.). You are aiming to let the examiner know how familiar you are with the topic.

In prompt 2, you focus more on how you would like to see some of the above technology make your life easier/better. Here the discussion begins to have a tighter focus.

Prompt 3 moves the discussion into general areas, quite often by asking you to consider the advantages and disadvantages of the topic, or the pros and cons, or just talking about a range of different views. In this case, you are discussing the pros and cons of *relying* on technology.

In prompt 4, you are usually given a statement made by someone which can be argued for and against, such as a controversial suggestion. You can either disagree, agree, or even a bit of both. Here, the discussion starts to get more demanding and you can really show your speaking skills, in particular how fluently you can help develop a discussion. The better you are at this, the wider your vocabulary will be and the way you structure your speaking will start to be impressive.

The final prompt tries to take the topic into the abstract – a sort of *What if?* question. You need to be able to talk about sophisticated matters here, as you move towards the end of the discussion. In this case, the abstract idea is that if we remove all technology we might have a better society. Prompt 5 is always open to debate.

At no point should your discussion be a general chat, so you and your examiner should use the five prompts to stay focused on the specific nature of the topic. For example, focusing on technology in the distant past would lead to an unproductive discussion.

TECHNOLOGY FOR THE FUTURE

Technology is always changing and is moving forwards at such a fast pace.
Discuss this topic with the examiner.

Use the following five prompts, in the order given below, to develop the conversation:

- the technology you currently use
- ways you would like to see technology improve
- the pros and cons of relying on technology
- the suggestion that technology just makes us all lazier and less healthy
- the idea the world would be a better place without technology.

You may introduce related ideas of your own to expand on these prompts.
Remember, you are not allowed to make any written notes.

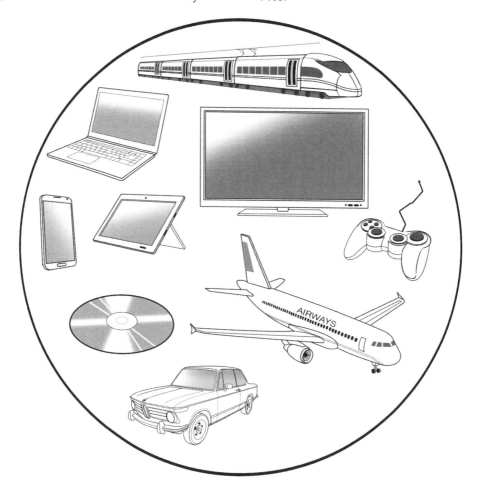

[Total: 30]

Self-assessment

In the speaking test there are three criteria which are used to arrive at a mark out of 30 for your performance in the test as a whole. We have converted these into easy-to-use checklists for you.

When you responded to the questions on the recording, did you feel that you:

My performance	Yes	No	If yes, …
Structure			
I used a wide range of accurate sentences and phrases, and felt confident all the way through.			Give yourself 9 or 10 marks.
I felt competent throughout and only struggled a little when I tried to be too complex.			Give yourself 7 or 8 marks.
I tended to stay with safer, simpler language so as not to make any mistakes.			Give yourself 5 or 6 marks.
I struggled and made too many mistakes in my spoken language.			Give yourself 3 or 4 marks.
Vocabulary			
I used a sophisticated range of words and used them at the right times.			Give yourself 9 or 10 marks.
I used a wide range of words and felt that it was sufficient to ensure a competent discussion.			Give yourself 7 or 8 marks.
I used an adequate range of words, but stumbled a little and used the wrong words at times.			Give yourself 5 or 6 marks.
I struggled more and hesitated to find the right words. I felt my vocabulary was limited.			Give yourself 3 or 4 marks.
Development and fluency			
I responded to all prompts confidently and felt that I spoke very clearly and naturally.			Give yourself 9 or 10 marks.
I responded to most prompts and only needed a little help at times.			Give yourself 7 or 8 marks.
I felt that the discussion was a partial success, but that I could have contributed more.			Give yourself 5 or 6 marks.
I struggled and gave too many short responses. I felt that the discussion was not successful and I struggled also to speak naturally and clearly.			Give yourself 3 or 4 marks.

By adding up your marks, you will arrive at a mark out of 30.

If your total mark is in the range:

- 25–30: you are doing really well
- 20–24: this is fine, but more practice is likely to help you a lot
- 15–19: it's a safe and secure performance
- 9–14: you are struggling a little and you should practise as much as you can by listening to lots of recorded discussions and taking part in as many discussions as you can. Start with shorter ones and gradually develop them.

Prepare for the examination

Paper 1 Reading and writing

EXERCISE 1 • Reading	
Type of task:	This is a reading exercise. You will read a text which will test your scanning skills. For your answers, you do not need to write full sentences, short responses are sufficient. You will have to understand what the writer of the text has implied as well as factual details. The format will be either a report or newspaper/magazine article.
You will be assessed on:	• identifying and retrieving facts and details • recognising and selecting relevant information • understanding what is implied in the text, such as the writer's feelings or opinions
Number of questions and marks:	This exercise will have a total of 13 marks. There is one final question which will have a maximum of 4 marks. <div style="text-align:right">Total of 13 marks</div>

Remember

Remember that it is a good idea to study the questions first to get an idea of what you need to look out for in the text. You should then scan the text by reading through quickly to try and find an idea or an expression that corresponds to a question. For example, in question (e) the expression *less active* carries the same idea as *sitting at a desk* in the text.

Don't forget that the questions are usually in the same order as the details in the text, so you should answer in sequence. You should also remember that the final question carries 4 marks and the information can be from anywhere in the text, so be prepared to look through the whole article again to find the answers.

Self-assessment

When you have finished the Exercise on pages 50–61, check your answers using the mark scheme at the back of the book. When you mark this question, the words underlined in the mark scheme must be in your answer to gain a mark. Don't forget that if you make a spelling or grammar mistake, it does not always mean that your answer is wrong.

PS 144

Exercise 1

Read the following article giving advice on how to lead a healthy life, and then answer the following questions.

Keeping the world healthy

The World Health Organisation (WHO) has provided written guidelines for what they consider as good health for all human beings. The organisation believes that we must not only be free from physical illness or sickness, we also have to be mentally healthy and enjoy life generally.

They emphasise that there are several key areas which can promote good quality of life and good health. Firstly, the environment in which we live is of great importance. Factors such as clean water and fresh air, adequate housing and safe communities have been found to contribute to good health. Studies show that a lack of neighbourhood recreational spaces, including a natural environment, leads to lower levels of personal health.

As individuals we can influence our own health by trying to live in a healthy way. It is important, for example, to eat a healthy diet, including a variety of plant-based and animal-based foods which provide nutrients to our bodies. Making healthy food choices can help lower our risk of heart disease and will contribute to maintaining a healthy weight. Physical exercise also enhances fitness and overall health by strengthening muscles and improving the cardiovascular system. By contrast, inactivity can contribute to health problems. As the number of tasks performed by machines has risen in most countries, more and more jobs now involve sitting at a desk in front of a computer.

A further essential area is sleep. Lack of sleep has been shown to relate with both the increased chance of becoming ill and slower recovery times from illness. In one study, people with chronic insufficient sleep, (six hours of sleep a night or less), were found to be four times more likely to catch a cold compared to those who reported sleeping for seven hours or more per night.

One further factor is the social structure of a person's life. The maintenance of strong social relationships have been linked to positive mental health and also longer life. Studies in America and Singapore reported that retired people who volunteer had significantly fewer depressive symptoms and better mental well-being and life satisfaction than non-volunteers.

Finally, to help us live long and healthy lives, health science is crucial and this consists of two main aspects. Firstly, the study and research of the body and health-related issues to understand how humans (and animals) function. Secondly, using that knowledge to improve health and to prevent and cure diseases. Health programmes in the workplace are increasingly being adopted by companies for their value in improving the health and well-being of their employees.

Achieving and maintaining health is a vital, ongoing process for everybody. Health care knowledge together with good personal planning and healthy lifestyle choices will give the world the best chance to stay healthy in the future.

(a) What has the WHO produced to help human beings stay healthy?

.... [1]

(b) What environmental factor can be a disadvantage to health?

.... [1]

(c) How can we make sure that we have enough nutrients?

.... [1]

(d) Which parts of the body benefit in particular from exercise? Give **two** details.

.... [1]

(e) Why have our jobs become less active?

.... [1]

(f) Who has more chance of catching colds?

.... [1]

(g) How can elderly people remain mentally healthy?

.... [1]

(h) What health care aspects need to work together for a healthy life? Give **two** details.

.... [2]

(i) What areas are vital in maintaining good health? Give **four** details.

....

....

....

....

....

....

.... [4]

[Total: 13]

EXERCISE 2 • Reading	
Type of task:	This is a reading exercise. You will read a text of approximately 650 words which will test all your reading skills. The task is a matching task: you will match statements to the person who has made the statement. It is likely that four different people will give accounts of their views on the same topic – but each person will present different views. Each person is likely to have written around 160 words, and the format will be diaries, blog entries or similar short pieces with a semi-formal register.
You will be assessed on:	• identifying and retrieving facts and details • recognising and selecting relevant information • understanding what is implied in the text, such as the writer's feelings or opinions
Number of questions and marks:	There are 10 short statements which you assign to one of four people. Each is worth 1 mark. Total of 10 marks

 Preparing for this type of question

In this practice exercise, you will see that there are four people who have a connection to science, but they all carry to very different jobs or roles in the field of science. Science, however, is what brings them all together. These people have never met each other but if they did meet they would be able to talk fluently about each other's experiences.

To help prepare for this exercise therefore, you could broaden your knowledge about topics by exploring different perspectives, particularly how people connect to a topic but in different ways. For example, surgeons, nurses, ambulance drivers and hospital managers all have a medical connection, but they all play very different roles within the profession. Think about what each role is what a person carrying out that role might say if you had a short interview with them. It's good practice for comparing and contrasting, and synthesising skills.

 **Exercise 2**

Read about four young people **(A-D)** who have written to a science website about their experiences. Then answer Question **10 (a)-(j)**.

SCIENCE TODAY

Four people share their thoughts on a science blog.

A I work in a laboratory which makes perfumes: I mix the ingredients to make the liquids which are eventually sold as perfumes by shops. It amazes me when I see so many different types of perfumes in the stores, as I know from my work that there are only about 50 different fragrances – the fragrance is the smell that each liquid has – so how they turn 50 fragrances into several hundred perfumes I will never know. You need very steady hands to do my job as we work with tiny amounts of liquids, transferring them and mixing them. Working in a lab means very long hours. I enjoy it a lot, but I didn't expect it would take so long to make a fragrance. I can't tell you how we do that as it's a scientific secret, but I can tell you that we are currently finishing a product which we have been perfecting for three years.

B I am an author but I am quite new to writing using the science fiction genre so I am also doing a lot of research into aspects of science. I guess my aim is to find a scientific truth but to stretch it so that it becomes fantasy. An example is where some characters I created melted when they went outside in the rain. They weren't people – I mean they weren't humans. They melted because they came from another planet and they hadn't yet adapted to Earth rain, as on their planet it is sunny all the time. I got the idea from a science magazine I read which showed that everything in the universe melts – that is, everything has its own melting point. I just played around with the idea of people melting. My next plot will be different. I am reading about robots made of metal, so there's probably no chance of them melting in the rain!

C I have just started teaching science to school children. This is my first job after spending three years studying science at university. What I find most challenging is not knowing about science, but teaching others to learn the science. When I was at university I was taught very advanced science and I found it quite easy to learn and understand. But now that I am teaching relatively easy science I find it hard to explain it at times. I prefer being in the classroom to being in a research unit, though – probably because I am practical person, rather than theoretical. Science can be very theoretical but I am more interested in carrying out experiments. I particularly like demonstrating how science works to my students: the more explosions I can make the better – controlled ones, of course.

D I am an amateur scientist, so I guess you could say it is my hobby. However, I take it very seriously and I am aiming to discover something new. I am interested in palaeontology, which is the study of fossils. I spend as much time as I can digging in the ground to look for old bones. I am part of a local group of similar-minded people and we are currently digging at a site in a forest. Last week we found our very first full fossil but unfortunately it wasn't a dinosaur. It was a fish, or rather the skeleton of a fish. We were excited at first, when the first few bones emerged, but then realised that we need to dig much deeper and work much harder to find something spectacular. Sometimes I dig on my own, which I don't particularly enjoy, but a few months ago, I found some old coins, and I got to keep them all to myself.

The questions below are about the people (A–D) who write about science.
For each question write the correct letter A, B, C or D on the line.
Which person ...

(a) takes science seriously but is not a specialist? ....   [1]

(b) uses science as the basis of story-writing? ....   [1]

(c) spends long periods of time in a laboratory? ....   [1]

(d) likes to use science to amaze and surprise people? ....   [1]

(e) finds it difficult sometimes to explain science? ....   [1]

(f) realises that creating things with science can be time-consuming? ....   [1]

(g) needs to be very still when carrying out the work? ....   [1]

(h) concerns themselves least with scientific facts? ....   [1]

(i) prefers the company of other people? ....   [1]

(j) sometimes keeps scientific knowledge to themselves? ....   [1]

[Total: 10]

PS 144

Self-assessment

9-10 marks: you have understood the approach needed for this type of exercise and you can locate specific detail, and infer attitudes and opinions of people.

7-8 marks: you have probably just made a couple if minor errors and this is nothing to worry about as you will improve with more practice.

5-6 marks: more practice is likely to help you refine these skills of synthesising and zooming in on the specific detail needed.

1-4 marks: you have struggled to identify what some of the people mean by what they say or by how they say it. More practice is needed.

EXERCISE 3 • Note-taking	
Type of task:	This is a note-taking exercise. You will need to read an article and write brief notes related to information in it. You will need to convey all key words and ideas in your answer, but will not need to write in full sentences.
You will be assessed on:	• identifying and retrieving facts and relevant information • recognising opinions and attitudes and the connections between related ideas
Number of questions and marks:	The Extended paper asks for 9 notes. Each note is worth 1 mark. Total of 9 marks

Remember

Remember to look at the headings on the notes template first, so that you have an idea of what information you are looking for in the reading text. Then when you read the text you can just focus on the details that fit each heading.

There is usually no need to change the words or expressions in the text when you write your answer.

Don't forget to write short notes, but make sure that all key words are included in your answer. You will need to find nine different details in all.

 **Exercise 3**

Read the following article about a family exercise class, and then complete the notes.

THE PARKOUR CLASS

I am here with my two children, four-year-old Alfie and three-year-old Jessica, to take part in a family class in parkour. This particular activity involves running around, climbing on, leaping off and rolling under obstacles, and usually takes place in towns or an urban environment. Its popularity has increased greatly in recent years and the number of participants has grown from being just teenagers and people in their twenties to enthusiasts of all ages.

Family parkour, with younger children, is different to adult-only parkour. It is more about making the time and space to play alongside the young children in your life, rather than exercising on your own. It is interesting because it quickly becomes clear that it is the adults who need to learn and not the children. In their short lives, the little ones have already successfully moved their way around obstacles at home and outdoors.

Each family class starts off with young and old dancing along to lively music and the whole idea is that it is the children who motivate the less-eager adults. The next activity involves some stretching exercises to warm-up, which is followed by the first game. Everybody has to think of an animal and move like it, which means shaping the body into strange positions and moving from one side of the room to the other. The children rush from point-to-point no matter whether they have chosen to be a lizard or a monkey. One result of this is that the adults have to increase their energy output to keep up with the children, rather than force the little ones to slow down to the speed of the adults.

Twenty minutes into the two-hour class, the adults are dripping with sweat. Alfie looks at me and focuses on my bright, red face and asks if I would like some of his water to drink. However, there is no time because we are already involved in the next activity, which is the mat-dragging game where the young ones sit on the mat and the adults have to drag them backwards and forwards repeatedly. This makes many of the adults out of breath, but this is not the finish of the activities because there still remains the key part of the class, the free running practice. This lasts about an hour and we have to use our body creatively to move past various obstacles (from chairs and tables, to small climbing frames and gymnastic equipment). The idea is to follow a specific route and get from A to B with the least effort, using the obstacles in our path. I am impressed by how confident the children are when they balance on a beam or hang off frames.

While the adults sit exhausted in corners during the break times, the children are desperate to return to their parkour playground. The activities stimulate the adults' enthusiasm and they smile and laugh along with the little ones. Is this kind of play actually the right thing for adults to be doing? The answer must be *yes*! You just have to let your little ones lead the way and start to crawl like a lizard, and then you will find yourself motivated by the excitement and variety of the activities.

You are going to talk to your local sports club about the family parkour classes.
Prepare some notes as the basis of your talk.

Make your notes under each heading.

The sequence of activities during the family class

- ....

- ....

- ....

- ....

Effects of the class activities on adults

- ....

- ....

- ....

- ....

- ....

[Total: 9]

Remember

Your answers need to be brief, but make sure that you include all the key details. Which of these two answers do you think is correct?

sit exhausted in corners at break times

Or

sit in corners at break times

If you think the first answer is correct, then you are right. The heading asks you to give details of the *effects* of the class activities and clearly the second answer does not contain that idea. The key word here is *exhausted* and is *essential* for a good answer.

Also, remember that you must only write one answer on each line.

Self-assessment

Now check your answers using the mark scheme at the end of the book. Remember that if there are two answers on a line you only mark the first answer.

Try to make sure that you copy words carefully and correctly from the text. However, if you do make a mistake in spelling or grammar, this does not automatically mean that your answer is wrong. When you assess each answer, you should look and see how serious the mistake is and decide if the meaning is still clear.

For example, *streching exercises* would give you 1 mark even though the spelling is wrong. Yet *dripping with sweet* would not get a mark because the spelling mistake means that the expression does not make sense.

EXERCISE 4 • Summary	
Type of task:	This is a summary writing exercise. You will need to read an article and write a summary about an aspect or aspects of it. You will need to convey as many relevant details as possible within a limit of either 80 or 120 words.
You will be assessed on:	• identifying and retrieving relevant information and ideas • communicating in writing clearly, accurately and appropriately • using and controlling grammatical structures including punctuation and spelling
Number of questions and marks:	For the Extended level paper reading and writing skills are assessed: 8 marks for reading and 8 marks for writing. Please see the checklist on page 64 to help you understand how these marks are awarded. Total of 16 marks

Remember

Remember that the main thing you should do before you start to write is to make sure that you read the wording of the question carefully, before looking at the text. You will then have a clear idea in your mind of what *exactly* is required. This will help you to concentrate only on the key information in the text and to ignore all the irrelevant details. The text is much longer than your summary, so there will be many details that you do not need to include.

Also, remember that you should try to change the words in the text and use your own expressions, but do make sure that your wording has exactly the same meaning as in the text.

 **Exercise 4**

Read the following article about freediving. Write a summary about what attracts people to this activity.

Your summary should be about 100 words long (and no more than 120 words long).
You should use your own words as far as possible.

You will receive up to 8 marks for the content of your summary, and up to 8 marks for the style and accuracy of your language.

FREEDIVING

Freediving is an activity where divers have to hold their breath underwater without using any breathing apparatus, such as oxygen tanks, to help them. It has become an increasingly popular sport and pastime over the past twenty years. It has its origins in ancient cultures, however, where freediving still exists today, not as a sport but as work. It is a technique used by fishermen in Asia and by brave Japanese divers who search for pearls in the ocean.

In today's world, freediving is often associated with competitive 'breath-hold' diving or competitive apnea. This is where competitors attempt to achieve great depths, times, or distances on a single breath. Enthusiasts love it because it gives them the chance to explore the limits of their ability and serious competitors pay as much attention to their diet, sleep patterns and stress levels as Olympic athletes.

I want to find out more about why people are increasingly finding this activity attractive and I have enrolled for a training session. There are four of us in the group led by a professional freediver from South America, who has been an instructor for over ten years. Today he is demonstrating the techniques that he uses when he dives deep underwater and stays there for minutes at a time. He explains, "Serious freedivers are attracted to this activity not so much as a competitive sport, but because they like the challenge of a different environment, and they just love the idea of living for the moment."

In the session, we are all practising holding our breath for as long as possible. Twenty seconds pass, then one minute as the first person in the group gives up and takes a breath. A few more seconds pass and then another person gives up. However, one man in his forties manages more than two minutes before he can take no more. These training sessions are vital because decompression sickness is common for freedivers and running out of oxygen can lead to unconsciousness. These dangers can be greatly reduced by self-awareness and responsibility learned through training.

However, it doesn't have to be so extreme. These days freediving is a leisure activity as well as a sport and people love it because it distracts them from the pressures of modern life. Freediving can be as simple as taking your snorkel from your mouth and heading underwater for as little as ten or twenty seconds at a time. "Freedivers are enthusiastic because they are discovering who they are," our instructor explains. "The effect on the freediver is very similar to that of yoga, producing a kind of very deep meditation which is a feeling that many love."

There are plenty of places to learn in the sea, under the care of an experienced instructor. There is a strong element of competition amongst those who are dedicated to the sport and they love it because it allows them to experience a sense of freedom. However, it is so much more than a competition to see who can dive the deepest and come back-up to the surface in one breath. Freedivers are enthusiastic about it because it allows them to take control of their own lives.

As the instructor says, "Why not put on a wetsuit, fins and goggles, get some professional instruction and I am sure that you will find the rewards can be as deep, beautiful and profound as the ocean itself."

....

....

....

....

....

....

....

....

....

....

....

....

....

....

....

....

....

....

....

....

[Total: 16]

Self-assessment

Checklist for marking use of language in summary writing

Here are some guidelines which you can used to arrive at a mark out of 8 for the **language** that you used in this exercise.

When I finished my written piece I felt...	Yes	No	If yes, ...
Language			
I was confident with my writing and tried very hard to change words and expressions in the text and use my own without making any mistakes. I also concentrated on making the details flow nicely with linking words.			Give yourself 7 or 8 marks.
I made some effort to change words here and there. I thought that my language was correct most of the time.			Give yourself 5 or 6 marks.
I was less confident about changing too many words from the original text and tended to stay with safer, simpler language so that I didn't make mistakes.			Give yourself 3 or 4 marks.
I didn't try to change any words and just simply copied the original. I wasn't able to include any linking words either and I felt that I made mistakes which would have made it hard for the reader to understand what I was trying to say.			Give yourself 2 or 4 marks.
I struggled with this exercise and could only copy some detail. I am not sure if the detail was correct or not, and my language had lots of mistakes.			Give yourself 1 mark.

As well as language marks, your summary may be awarded marks for each correct **content** detail that you convey. These details are listed in the mark scheme at the back of the book.

You do not have to use the same words as in the mark scheme – in fact it is better if you use your own expressions – but you do have to convey the key details of each point.

How about practising to see if you can change the wording of the content points on the mark scheme? There are 8 points, so try and use your own words to convey each idea, but make sure that you do not lose the precise meaning of each point.

EXERCISE 5 • Writing	
Type of task:	This is a writing exercise. You will need to write a piece, such as an email or a letter to a friend or family member. Your style of writing or register should be informal.
You will be assessed on:	• writing and developing original ideas and feelings effectively • communicating with accurate grammar, punctuation and style
Number of questions and marks:	There is just one main task, but there are three bullet points to consider. You must write something for all three bullet points. <div style="text-align:right">Total of 16 marks</div>

Remember

Consider the following points before you start:

- Think about the person who is receiving your letter or email because this will make sure that you write in the correct style. This question usually asks you to write to a friend or family member, so your writing should be *informal*.
- Look carefully at the wording of the three bullet points, such as *explain*, *describe* and *say*, making sure you think about what you are expected to do. You should plan to write a paragraph about each bullet point.
- Remember to include a brief introduction and conclusion, two or three short sentences will be enough for each.
- Don't forget to attempt more ambitious language and try to use rhetorical questions and exclamations, to add variety and life to your writing.

What do you think of this as an introduction?

> Hi Miriam,
>
> How are you doing back there in London? I hope that you and your parents are fine. What about your lovely little brother? Is he still running all over the place and shouting and screaming? What about your school? I heard that you are doing well and are at the top of the class. Well done, you! I have recently taken up a new hobby.

What are the good points? Firstly, the style is very informal and friendly. The student has used rhetorical questions and an exclamation mark to give variety to the writing.

What is not so good? If you think it is too long, then you are right. There are almost 70 words here, nearly half of the total word requirement for the email. There are too many questions and there is too much information.

What would be better? The first two sentences are fine, but we can certainly leave out the question and statement about the brother. Then the question about the school could simply be replaced with I heard that you are doing well at school. Well done, you!

Finally, the sentence about the new hobby addresses the first bullet point and should be at the start of the next paragraph.

Exercise 5

You have recently started a new hobby.

Write an email to a friend about this experience.

In your email you should:

- explain how you became interested in the hobby;
- say what it involves;
- describe how you feel about it so far.

Your email should be between 150 and 200 words long. Do not write an address.

The pictures above may give you some ideas, and you should try to use some ideas of your own.

You will receive up to 8 marks for the content of your email, and up to 8 marks for the style and accuracy of your language.

[Total: 16]

Self-assessment

Two criteria are used to mark this exercise: **content** and **language**, both of which have a maximum mark of 8.

We have converted these into easy-to-use checklists for you.

When I finished my written piece I felt...	Yes	No	If yes, …
Content			
I developed my ideas very well, writing lots of extra detail. I made sure that I referred to the reader all the time, with a correct formal or informal style. I thought that the reader would find my writing very enjoyable.			Give yourself 8 marks.
I completed all the parts of the task and added some extra ideas and detail. I remembered who I was writing for and wrote in a style that was appropriate.			Give yourself 6 or 7 marks.
My style of writing was OK and I made sure that my piece was always about the subject, but I was not able to add much extra detail.			Give yourself 5 marks.
I wasn't sure that I was successful in keeping to the topic all the time. I didn't have too many ideas and felt that I wrote some things which were not really relevant.			Give yourself 4 marks.
I didn't really think about who was going to read the piece and wrote in the wrong style. I also felt that I was short of ideas and repeated myself at times.			Give yourself 2 or 3 marks.
Language			
I was confident with my writing and used a wide range of very accurate language and even managed to include some good idioms. I made sure that my verb tenses were all correct. All in all, I thought that I made very few errors.			Give yourself 8 marks.
I tried to use some more unusual words and expressions and think that I was generally accurate with them. I remembered to use paragraphs to divide the different ideas that I had.			Give yourself 6 or 7 marks.
I tended to stay with safer, simpler language so that I didn't make mistakes.			Give yourself 4 or 5 marks.
I found the writing hard, made too many mistakes and maybe the person reading my piece would have had problems at times trying to understand it.			Give yourself 2 or 3 marks.

Now add up your marks from the two checklists to arrive at a mark out of 16.

If your total mark is in the range:

- 14–16: you are doing really well
- 10–13: this is fine, but more practice is likely to help you a lot
- 7–9: it's a safe and secure performance
- 0–6: you are struggling a little and you should practise as much as you can developing more ideas and working hard to get your verb tenses correct. Start with short paragraphs one at a time and gradually develop them.

EXERCISE 6 • Writing	
Type of task:	This is a writing exercise. You will need to write a piece, such as an article for a school magazine or a letter to a newspaper. Your style of writing or register should be formal and you should try to persuade the reader of your opinions.
You will be assessed on:	• writing and developing original ideas, feelings and opinions effectively • communicating with accurate grammar, punctuation and style
Number of questions and marks:	There is just one main task, but there are two brief prompts to consider. You may use the ideas in these prompts and develop them, or think of your own ideas. <div align="right">Total of 16 marks</div>

Remember

You should always think about who you are writing to and using a more formal style. Try to have three or four different ideas at the most and develop them, rather than having a lot of disconnected thoughts with no real detail.

It doesn't matter if you are 'for' or 'against' the argument, or if you prefer to give a balanced view for both sides. The main thing is to support your ideas with plenty of detail and use words and expressions which persuade the reader to believe you.

You should plan to write at least two paragraphs to express your views and don't forget to include a brief introduction and conclusion.

Which of these styles of writing do you think is better?

> 1) I like supermarkets and I don't like small shops. Supermarkets are more convenient because they are big and have plenty of things to buy. I do think that the service is very good in the small shops, however, and so I often go there because I know the sales assistant very well and we always talk to each other.

> 2) In my opinion, there is no doubt that supermarkets are much better than small shops. You only have to look at the breathtaking variety of goods on offer to realise that the small shops can never compete with the huge range of products. Moreover, they cannot match the prices of the supermarkets because the chain stores are able to buy large quantities of each item.

I think that you will agree that the second piece is better, but why?

- In the second piece, the language is much more ambitious, you should always try to think of stronger words than *good* and *big*.
- The first example uses the ideas in the prompts and does not develop them, whereas the second piece has independent ideas.
- In the second example, the writer appears more passionate about the topic. The writer of the first piece does not seem very convinced and makes a case for both sides of the argument. The detail about the shop assistant is quite weak.

▤ Exercise 6

Your local newspaper is planning a series of articles with the title: '*How supermarkets affect small food shops in our town*'.

Here are two comments about this idea:

"Supermarkets are so convenient."

"I like the personal service in the small shops."

Write a letter to your local newspaper giving your views.

Your letter should be between 150 and 200 words long.

The comments above may give you some ideas, and you should try to use some ideas of your own.

You will receive up to 8 marks for the content of your article, and up to 8 marks for the style and accuracy of your language.

....

....

....

....

....

....

....

....

....

....

....

....

....

....

....

....

....

....

....

....

....

[Total: 16]

Self-assessment

Two criteria are used to mark this exercise: **content** and **language**, both of which have a maximum mark of 8.

We have converted these into easy-to-use checklists for you.

When I finished my written piece I felt...	Yes	No	If yes, …
Content			
I developed my ideas very well, writing lots of extra detail. I made sure that I referred to the reader all the time, with a correct formal or informal style. I thought that the reader would find my writing very enjoyable.			Give yourself 8 marks.
I completed all the parts of the task and added some extra ideas and detail. I remembered who I was writing for and wrote in a style that was appropriate.			Give yourself 6 or 7 marks.
My style of writing was OK and I made sure that my piece was always about the subject, but I was not able to add much extra detail.			Give yourself 5 marks.
I wasn't sure that I was successful in keeping to the topic all the time. I didn't have too many ideas and felt that I wrote some things which were not really relevant.			Give yourself 4 marks.
I didn't really think about who was going to read the piece and wrote in the wrong style. I also felt that I was short of ideas and repeated myself at times.			Give yourself 2 or 3 marks.
Language			
I was confident with my writing and used a wide range of very accurate language and even managed to include some good idioms. I made sure that my verb tenses were all correct. All in all, I thought that I made very few errors.			Give yourself 8 marks.
I tried to use some more unusual words and expressions and think that I was generally accurate with them. I remembered to use paragraphs to divide the different ideas that I had.			Give yourself 6 or 7 marks.
I tended to stay with safer, simpler language so that I didn't make mistakes.			Give yourself 4 or 5 marks.
I found the writing hard, made too many mistakes and maybe the person reading my piece would have had problems at times trying to understand it.			Give yourself 2 or 3 marks.

Now add up your marks from the two checklists to arrive at a mark out of 16.

If your total mark is in the range:

- 17–19: you are doing really well
- 14–16: this is fine, but more practice is likely to help you a lot
- 11–13: it's a safe and secure performance
- 0–10: you are struggling a little and you should practise as much as you can developing more ideas and working hard to get your verb tenses correct. Start with short paragraphs one at a time and gradually develop them.

Paper 2 Listening

EXERCISE 1	
Type of task:	There are four short extracts. Each of the four has a different theme. Announcements or brief dialogues (formal or informal) are often used. The questions require short answers, no longer than three words each.
You will be assessed on:	• identifying and retrieving facts and details
Number of questions and marks:	There are four questions, but each one is split into two separate parts. Each question is worth 2 marks. Total of 8 marks

Remember

You can use up to three words for each answer, so it is acceptable to use one or two words. You should aim to use as few words as possible to convey your answer – so where one word is enough, just use one!

You can use synonyms if they have exactly the same meaning, and you don't need to worry too much about spelling and grammar, as slight errors will be accepted if the meaning is clear enough.

Self-assessment

Complete the questions on page 75, and then check your answers using the mark scheme at the back of the book. If you see this symbol / it means that any of the list of responses is fine and would get a mark. If you see a word underlined, it means that the word, or an exact synonym, must be in the answer. In some cases the mark scheme would include answers that would *not* be accepted, and some awkward spellings that *would* be accepted. If a word appears in brackets ( ) then it might be used, but it doesn't have to be. Try to learn these marking rules as it will help you do better in your exam by guiding you to look for exactly what questions are asking for.

P S 146

 **Exercise 1**

You will hear four short recordings. Answer each question on the line provided. Write no more than **three** words for each answer.

You can play the recording twice.

1 **(a)** What facility is available to children under 16?

.... [1]

(b) When is a member allowed to have the free one-hour session?

.... [1]

2 **(a)** How many electric guitars are in Brian's collection?

.... [1]

(b) What is the slight concern with Brian's favourite guitar?

.... [1]

3 **(a)** Where does the husband suggest taking his wife?

.... [1]

(b) Why isn't the wife keen at first?

.... [1]

4 **(a)** Why does the women need to go to the pathology department?

.... [1]

(b) Where does the blue line lead to?

.... [1]

[Total: 8]

EXERCISE 2	
Type of task:	This is a semi-formal talk and you will be asked to fill in a notepad using one or two words only.
You will be assessed on:	• identifying and retrieving facts and details • understanding and selecting relevant information
Number of questions and marks:	There will be eight notes for you to fill in, each worth 1 mark. Some of the notes are provided, so you only need to write in the empty gaps to complete the other, remaining notes. Total of 8 marks

Remember

Listening for specific information is the key skill being tested. There are two levels of this: simply locating a detail, but also being able to select a *relevant* detail from some options. You are likely to score more marks if you can pick out these relevant details. Look carefully at the grid on the exam paper where you write your answers and notice that they are notes, rather than full sentences. The detail you need to fill in can come at the beginning, middle or end of the note. So pinning the detail down to one or two words is important.

Self-assessment

Complete the questions on page 76, and then check your answers using the mark scheme at the back of the book. When you assess your own answers remember not to be too strict with your spelling. The main objective is to get the right detail. For example, if you've had trouble spelling *lens* as long as the sound your word creates is similar, you should give yourself a mark. Therefore, if you put *lenz* that would be fine. Also, if you put *payshents* for *patients* that too would be accepted.

A good way to attempt spellings is to use the same number of syllables as in the word you have heard. *Artificial* is a good example of this – *AR-TI-FI-CIAL*. Then with the word *degenerate*, an attempt such as *DE-JEN-ERR-EIGHT* would also work. Hopefully your spelling will be better than that!

Exercise 2

You will hear a talk given by an eye specialist at a hospital. Listen to the talk and complete the notes below. Write **one** or **two** words or a **number** in each gap.

You can play the talk twice.

THE SHANGHAI EYE HOSPITAL

A team at the hospital has been carrying out research for a new treatment to restore lost vision.

The hospital

Specialises in eye treatment

One of .... eye research hospitals in China

Treatment for patients with cataracts

Recent breakthrough in cataract cases in children

Over 50% of cases in children .... are caused by cataracts

A cataract is when the lens of the eye becomes cloudy

Current treatment uses an .... lens

A tiny .... removes the cataract

Stem cells are then added to help rebuild the lens

Tests and trials

Started with children

A child's eye is likely to .... faster than an adult eye

Adult trial will involve .... lasting two years

A smaller trial group will focus on .... patients

Other planned research

Exploring a relationship with hospitals in specialising in other eye conditions

Schedule for the day

Tour of the hospital facilities

Demonstration in the ....

Meet ten very special patients

[Total: 8]

EXERCISE 3	
Type of task:	There will be some short, informal monologues and you will try to match each speaker to the appropriate opinion that is expressed in the monologue.
You will be assessed on:	• recognising and understanding ideas, opinions and attitudes • recognising the connections between related ideas • understanding what is implied but not actually stated, e.g. gist, relationships between speakers, speaker's purpose, speaker's intention • working out a speaker's feelings, situation or place
Number of questions and marks:	There are six speakers and seven opinions given as monologues. One of the opinions is extra and is not used. There is 1 mark for each of the 6 correct matches. Total of 6 marks

Remember

The statements on the exam paper will be shortened versions of what each speaker says – short summaries if you like – but some of the words will have been changed from what you hear in the recording. This is to also test your understanding of the gist (general idea) of what each of them is saying. Some of the opinions are similar, but also have a clear difference. Listen carefully for what is *different* as this is likely to feature on the exam paper.

Self-assessment

Complete the activity on page 78, then check your answers using the mark scheme at the back of the book. When you mark your own work for this question it might be helpful to remember that some of what each speaker says will overlap, and therefore you might be considering two or three statements for a speaker. However, *all* of what is in the statement must match what the speaker says in the recording. Perhaps give yourself a second option when you write your answers down (i.e. I'm pretty sure it's Statement B, but my second guess would be D.). Then see how many second choices were actually correct.

148

 Exercise 3

6 You will hear six people talking about their views on taking holidays. For each of Speakers 1 to 6, choose from the list, **A** to **G**, which opinion each speaker expresses. Write the letter in the box. Use each letter only once. There is one extra letter which you do not need to use.

Speaker 1 ____

A I think it's important to be as adventurous as possible on holiday.

Speaker 2 ____

B I prefer a calm and peaceful location for a holiday, and I need a climate which complements this.

Speaker 3 ____

C I prefer noisy holidays with lots of people around. I like to be part of the crowd.

Speaker 4 ____

D I prefer to travel alone while on holiday.

Speaker 5 ____

E The main reason for taking a holiday should be to relax.

Speaker 6 ____

F I think the main aim of a holiday is to appreciate the local area and learn something about the local people.

G I don't see a holiday as a need to escape work. In fact, I think a holiday can inspire you.

[Total: 6]

EXERCISE 4	
Type of task:	You will listen to a semi-formal discussion between two speakers.
You will be assessed on:	• recognising and understanding ideas, opinions and attitudes • recognising the connections between related ideas • understanding what is implied but not actually stated, e.g. gist, relationships between speakers, speaker's purpose, speaker's intention • working out a speaker's feelings, situation or place
Number of questions and marks:	There are eight questions worth 1 mark each. They are all multiple choice questions and you will choose from three options: A, B or C. One of these is a distractor, which means it is there to purposefully lead you away from the correct answer. Total of 8 marks

Remember

The questions are in multiple choice format, so you will need to think carefully about which of the three answers is the *most* accurate. Look carefully for answers which are not quite right or which have some of the required detail, but not all of it, or answers which have some correct detail and then an incorrect detail. Therefore, you will need to look carefully at all three options and deduce which is the most appropriate one. Don't jump in too quickly!

Self-assessment

Complete the questions on pages 80–81, then check your answers using the mark scheme at the back of the book. This question tests your ability to listen as well as work out or infer what a person is saying, so it is just as much a test of locating what has actually been said. Therefore, the first few questions are likely to focus on finding facts and numbers and choosing the correct information or detail from the three choices, so listen carefully!

Later on, the questions will see how well you have understood what the person is thinking, so you will need to listen for the clues (i.e. what the speaker *implies*).

148

 Exercise 4

7   You will hear a TV presenter talking to Lim, who is a fan of the *Star Wars* films. Listen to their conversation and look at the questions. For each question choose the correct answer, **A**, **B** or **C**, and put a tick (✓) in the appropriate box.

You can play the talk twice.

(a)   When was the first *Star Wars* film released?

   A   1970   ☐

   B   1977   ☐

   C   1907   ☐   [1]

(b)   The original film was very successful and it earned the producers

   A   just under 11 million dollars   ☐

   B   more than 775 million dollars   ☐

   C   approximately 764 million dollars   ☐   [1]

(c)   *Star Wars* was one of the films that experimented with

   A   computer graphics   ☐

   B   SGI   ☐

   C   computers   ☐   [1]

(d)   What does Lim find most impressive about the bird-like creatures?

   A   They make loud and piercing noises.   ☐

   B   They have 1.8 metre body lengths and 1.25 metre wingspans.   ☐

   C   They feed on electrical energy.   ☐   [1]

(e)   What was special about the *Star Tours* experience?

   A   It was an idea that Hollywood had.   ☐

   B   It was an idea that the maker of *Star Wars* had.   ☐

   C   It was an idea that Disneyland had.   ☐   [1]

(f) How have *Star Tours* and theme parks added to the fans' experience?

    A They get to meet Mr Lucas, who created them. ☐

    B They get to travel in a *Star Wars* space craft. ☐

    C They get to go on an adventure from Tokyo to the USA. ☐ [1]

(g) Which statement is true?

    A Lim has been to one theme park in Tokyo and another in the United States. ☐

    B Lim has been to only one theme park in Tokyo in 2015. ☐

    C Lim has been to only one theme park, but they also exist around the world. ☐ [1]

(h) The mood of the event in Singapore could be described as

    A colourful and lively. ☐

    B atmospheric, but a little uninspiring. ☐

    C vibrant, but not well attended. ☐ [1]

[Total: 8]

EXERCISE 5	
Type of task:	There are two parts to this question, Part A and Part B, but they are connected. You will hear a talk for Part A, given by one person, and in Part B, you will hear a dialogue between two people about the talk (i.e. picking up on various aspects of the talk).
	The task for Part A requires you to complete short notes with one or two words. The task for Part B requires you to also use only one or two words, but to complete gaps in sentences.
	The talk will be of a semi-formal nature, but the discussion afterwards is likely to be informal.
You will be assessed on:	• identifying and retrieving facts and details
	• understanding and selecting relevant information
	• recognising and understanding ideas, opinions and attitudes
	• recognising the connections between related ideas
	• understanding what is implied but not actually stated, e.g. gist, relationships between speakers, speaker's purpose, speaker's intention
	• working out a speaker's feelings, situation or place
Number of questions and marks:	In Part A there are five notes to fill in worth 1 mark each.
	In Part B there are five sentences to complete worth 1 mark each.
	Total of 10 marks

Remember

There are two parts to this question. In the first part, you will hear a talk which has a semi-formal feel to it, so there will be some facts and details given by the speaker that you could be asked to locate. In the second part, you will hear a dialogue between two people who have listened to the talk. This will be more informal and you will hear both speakers express their views and opinions. Therefore, you are likely to be asked what their views and opinions are, and in some cases, work out (infer) what they are.

 **Exercise 5**

8 (a) You will hear a woman, called Su Lin, giving a talk about a new fitness park, which has opened in her home town in Vietnam. Listen to the talk and complete the notes in Part A. Write **one** or **two** words only in each gap.

149

You can play the talk twice.

The development of the fitness park

The aim was to provide a free facility for the people in the city

It took .... to construct the park

The plot of land was vacant for many years

Problems to resolve

It was usually covered with weeds, bamboo and other flora

It was necessary to .... breeds of snake

Continued neglect meant the park was usually overgrown

Funding the new fitness park

An investment group proposed building ....

The city council agreed to the fitness park idea

Funds were provided by ....

Specialist considerations

Excavation experts needed to make sure the ground was solid

Architects were brought in to design the standing buildings

A membrane was used to .... the gym equipment

Other uses of the park

Events and gatherings where people can meet and enjoy food and drink

[Total: 5]

Exercise 5

8 (b) Now listen to a conversation between two tourists, Jason and Anita, about their first visit to the new fitness park. Complete the sentences in Part B. Write one or two words only in each gap.

You can play the conversation twice.

The fitness park as a tourist attraction

(a) Jason is happy that they didn't go to the ....

(b) Jason thinks that .... will find the fitness park enjoyable.

(c) Anita thinks that governments should ensure that local people .... from building projects in cities.

(d) The two agree that not allowing .... is likely to be a cultural matter.

(e) It would seem that one of the rules is aimed at .... local food sellers.

[Total: 5]

Self-assessment

Part A

You can use one or two words only, and you can use synonyms, but be careful if you do to make sure your new words mean exactly the same as the ones used in the recording. If you used *move* instead of *relocate* this is not quite the same thing; but if you used *cover* instead of *protect*, this would be allowed as synonymous. An underlined word must be used in the answer. Therefore, if you omitted *local* then you wouldn't receive the mark, as the fact that it was local businesses which funded the project is important.

Part B

Remember that in this section you are given full sentences, rather than notes. So try to ensure that what you add to the gaps helps create a full and proper sentence (i.e. the resulting sentence must flow, and the words inserted must be grammatically accurate). You can still be slightly out with your spelling, but the grammar must be secure. For example, in the recording you hear the word *protect*, but in the gap you will need to use *protecting* to show full and complete understanding. Our advice is to use only one word for each sentence in this section, if you can, rather than two. In this practice question, one word works for all five sentences.

Paper 3 Speaking

EXERCISE 1 • Speaking	
Type of task:	There are 10 test cards with 10 different themes. However, your examiner will choose the topic/theme and present the card to you. You are not allowed to choose your own test card. You can look at the card for a few minutes and think of what you might say and how the discussion might develop. The main part of the exam lasts for 6–9 minutes and it is during this part that you will be assessed. Before you are given the card, there is a 2–3 minute warm-up during which the examiner will help settle you down with some general conversation.
You will be assessed on:	• **Structure** The range you use and how accurately you control them. Think of this as the accuracy of your spoken language. • **Vocabulary** How precise and competent your use of words is. At the higher level, can you convey shades of meaning? At a secure level, is your vocabulary sufficient to convey your ideas clearly? • **Development** Your ability to sustain and expand upon the discussion. At the higher level, can you respond to changes of direction and can you contribute at some length? • **Fluency** This is really a measure of how clear your pronunciation and intonation is. Does your speaking flow naturally, using appropriate tone, emphasis, stressing of certain words, etc.?
Number of questions and marks:	You will be presented with a single test card which has a main theme to discuss, followed by five bullet points to help you contribute and develop the conversation. Each of the five prompts serves a different purpose and together they help build the discussion, making it more sophisticated as it progresses. The five prompts can be thought of as questions, though on the card they are given as statements. The examiner will use all five prompts. You will be awarded up to: 10 marks for structure 10 marks for vocabulary 10 marks for development and fluency Total of 30 marks

Remember

There are always five prompts and you and your examiner are expected to work your way through them, discussing each one in turn. The prompts are designed to move from the personal (about you) and less demanding, through the general (pros and cons etc.), to more controversial, suggestive and abstract as the discussion ends. This is called *scaffolding* and aims to *develop* the discussion. One of your assessment criteria measures how good you are at playing a part in this development.

Open and closed questions

It's important that the examiner asks you 'open questions' so that you can respond with more than just a 'yes' or 'no'. You should practise by using some open questions and we have provided some below, which could be asked in connection to the test card in this section. It's easy to convert a 'closed question' into an open question. For example:

> "Do you like gym classes with a group of people exercising, or do you prefer to exercise by yourself?"

This is closed because you only have two potential responses *with a group* or *on my own*. Therefore, closed questions do not always end up with 'yes' or 'no' answers. We think this is a much better way to ask the same question:

> "What is it about exercising with a group of people, all together in the room, that you like or dislike?"

As you work through this second practice exam test card think about these open and closed questions. It will be much easier for you to be successful if you know the difference and can work towards using open questions. We have included two closed questions for you, so see if you can spot them on the recording!

Questions posed as statements

Sometimes, and probably as the discussion is developing with prompts 3, 4 and 5, your examiner will *pose* a question as a statement, inviting you to pick up on what he or she has said and move the discussion along. This is allowed, and is in fact a good examining technique as it lets you take a part in the direction of the discussion. Here's an example of how it might work. The examiner might say:

> "I think that people just have to start taking more responsibility for their own health and well-being. There are too many people being tempted to do unhealthy things."

So there is no question there. It is a statement, but it is intended as a provocative one, which means that you should respond with your point of view. You would usually agree, disagree or present both sides of the issue being raised.

Listen out in the recording for some examples of these types of 'questions as statements', as we have built some into the discussion about healthy living.

HEALTHY LIVING FOR THE FUTURE

Being as healthy as possible is probably an aim for the majority of people around the world. Discuss this topic with the examiner.

Use the following five prompts, in the order given below, to develop the conversation:
- ways that you personally try to stay healthy
- your views on generally how healthy people are around you
- the two sides of the health issue: how easy it is for some, but how challenging for others
- the suggestion that it is easier for wealthier people to stay healthy than poorer people
- whether the human population is in fact making itself unhealthy just by the way it is evolving.

You may introduce related ideas of your own to expand on these prompts.
Remember, you are not allowed to make any written notes.

[Total: 30]

Self-assessment

In the speaking test there are three criteria which are used to arrive at a mark out of 30 for your performance in the test as a whole.

We have converted these into easy-to-use checklists for you.

My performance	Yes	No	If yes, ...
Structure			
I used a wide range of accurate sentences and phrases, and felt confident all the way through.			Give yourself 9 or 10 marks.
I felt competent throughout and only struggled a little when I tried to be too complex.			Give yourself 7 or 8 marks.
I tended to stay with safer, simpler language so not to make any mistakes.			Give yourself 5 or 6 marks.
I struggled and made too many mistakes in my spoken language.			Give yourself 3 or 4 marks.
Vocabulary			
I used a sophisticated range of words and used them at the right times.			Give yourself 9 or 10 marks.
I used a wide range of words and felt that it was sufficient to ensure a competent discussion.			Give yourself 7 or 8 marks.
I used an adequate range of words, but stumbled a little and used the wrong words at times.			Give yourself 5 or 6 marks.
I struggled more and hesitated to find the right words. I felt my vocabulary was limited.			Give yourself 3 or 4 marks.
Development and fluency			
I responded to all prompts confidently and felt that I spoke very clearly and naturally.			Give yourself 9 or 10 marks.
I responded to most prompts and only needed a little help at times.			Give yourself 7 or 8 marks.
I felt that the discussion was a partial success, but that I could have contributed more.			Give yourself 5 or 6 marks.
I struggled and gave too many short responses. I felt that the discussion was not successful and I struggled also to speak naturally and clearly.			Give yourself 3 or 4 marks.

Now add up your marks to arrive at a mark out of 30.

If your total mark is in the range:

- 25–30: you are doing really well
- 20–24: this is fine, but more practice is likely to help you a lot
- 15–19: it's a safe and secure performance
- 9–14: you are struggling a little and you should practise as much as you can by listening to lots of recorded discussions and taking part in as many discussions as you can. Start with shorter ones and gradually develop them.

Practice for the examination
Paper 1 Reading and writing

 Exercise 1

Read the following article about a studio which produces computer animated films, and then answer the following questions.

PIXAR STUDIOS AND THE FILM *TOY STORY*

Pixar Animation Studios, or simply Pixar, is an American computer animation film studio, based in California. Pixar started in the 1970s when they employed computer scientists who shared ambitions about creating the world's first computer-animated films. The studio has since grown into one of the most successful in the world.

During the 1990s and 2000s, Pixar developed a method of working known as the "Pixar Braintrust" in which the directors, writers and artists at the studio comment on each other's ideas and criticise each other's work on a regular basis, in order to ensure that the final product has been thoroughly tested at all stages. Pixar has now produced more than 15 films, beginning with *Toy Story 1* in 1995, the first-ever computer-animated feature film. The studio's feature films have since made over 9.5 billion dollars worldwide.

What was the thinking behind the idea for the film *Toy Story 1*? The studio realised that humans were difficult to create in animated form and so it was decided to tell the story from the point of view of the toys in a boy's bedroom. The two main characters are Woody, a cowboy, and Buzz Lightyear, a spaceman. Originally *Toy Story 1* was about a little toy which gets left on the side of a road and goes on a journey to find its owners. Finally, however, the studio decided that it should be a story about toys with different personalities who become friends. In the first trials, the cowboy (Woody) was a very mean and unpleasant character, but the actor Tom Hanks, who was the voice of Woody, said that he found this difficult because Woody was supposed to be the most popular toy in the boy's bedroom. As the film progressed, the personality of Woody became less harsh and friendlier.

The original film was an incredible success and the difficult task for the studio was then to produce something just as good, if not better, as a follow-up or sequel. There have since been two more *Toy Story* films and all of them have been very successful.

Pixar Studios are now trying to produce three films every two years and the idea is to make an original every year and a sequel every other year. Their characters are always different, for example, the film *Ratatouille* features a rat in a kitchen, and the film *UP* explored the relationship between an old man and a boy scout. Often when a company has a huge hit film they quickly start developing a sequel, a follow-up based closely on the successful original. One criticism of sequels is that they lack new content, but generally audiences love them and they are successful. All Pixar films have been computer-animated features, but *WALL-E*, about a rubbish-crushing robot, is the only Pixar feature so far which is not completely animated, as it contains a small amount of live-action film.

Pixar is a studio with a small group of enthusiastic film-makers who just want to keep on producing big films containing very personal stories.

(a) What did the first group of Pixar workers have in common?

.... [1]

(b) How did the Braintrust ensure that their work was the best that they could produce?

.... [1]

(c) Why did the film studio choose toys for their first feature film?

.... [1]

(d) What theme was eventually decided for *Toy Story 1*?

.... [1]

(e) What was the problem that Tom Hanks had with the character of Woody? Give **two** details.

....

.... [2]

(f) What was the challenge for Pixar with their second film?

.... [1]

(g) How often does Pixar plan to make a follow-up film?

.... [1]

(h) What is a possible disadvantage of follow-up films?

.... [1]

(i) Name **four** Pixar films and their main characters.

....

....

....

.... [4]

[Total: 13]

Exercise 2

Read the article about four people **(A–D)** who come from very different cultures. Then answer Question **10 (a)–(j)**.

WHAT A WONDERFUL WORLD

Four people contribute to a web-based discussion forum, sharing their thoughts on cultures and customs.

A When I saw this discussion group about customs and cultures I just had to share some aspects of my own culture with you all. I'm from New Zealand, and when we greet each other we rub each other's noses! But not everybody in my culture does this. My family is a traditional Maori family and it's much more common to rub noses in the Maori culture. I found out that in Japan it's common to bow to each other, and in Tibet some people say hello by sticking their tongues out! When I was a young child I remember a funny moment when a guest came to our house and greeted my father but the guest closed his eyes at the last moment. It wasn't so much a nose rub as a nose to forehead rub. But now that I am older I want to keep this tradition going as I feel strongly that these types of customs should not die out.

B I regard myself as a global citizen. I was born in the United States, but since I graduated two years ago I have been travelling around the world. As I post this message on this forum, I am currently in Bangkok, the capital city of Thailand. I have been here for three months, to absorb the rich culture they have here. I like the way Thai people are open and friendly, and how keen they are to preserve their open culture but welcome lots of other cultures too. Before I got here, I spent two months in Moscow and Russian culture is very different to Thai culture. I think it might be something to do with the climates in the two places – one is very hot, the other can be very cold. I leave Thailand soon to travel to France, and I expect a different set of customs again. My aim is to visit more places to have enough experience to write a book about how we can all learn from these very different cultures.

C I was watching a TV show last week that suggested I was a *global nomad* and I was quite surprised to hear that. I think a nomad is someone who has no home, and likes to wander about – like a person in an ancient tribe. I know there are nomadic people still around today but I wouldn't describe myself as a nomad. I am, however, a TCK – *third culture kid*. I'm 17 years old and I am currently at college in China. I am with my parents who are both working here. My mother is Swedish and my father is French, so that makes me quite a mixture. I speak Swedish and French at home, but English at school; and I am now learning Chinese as well. The TV show also suggested that I don't have a sense of belonging to any one culture as I move about too much. Not true! I feel like I belong to at least three different cultures.

D British culture is very hard to define. I am from England and have lived here all my life. My country is very multi-cultural. In most of our cities we have people from a wide range of different cultural backgrounds and you can see this when you walk around the streets with the variety of restaurants, religious places, and the languages you hear people talking. In contrast, being British can be quite a challenge as we have a long history of having a mono-culture - that is a single culture - so sometimes we have culture clashes between British people and people from other cultures. Being British can mean that we do some very odd things. For example, we solve all our problems by sitting down and having a cup of tea; and we always form an orderly queue in shops. Oh, and we love to wash our cars and mow our garden lawns on a Sunday morning.

The questions below are about the people (A–D) who send messages to a forum.
For each question write the correct letter A, B, C or D on the line.
Which person …

(a)   thinks that the weather can influence a culture? ....   [1]

(b)   feels that their culture can be stuck in the past? ....   [1]

(c)   holds onto traditional cultures the most? ....   [1]

(d)   has the weakest connection to a single culture? ....   [1]

(e)   is interested in the different customs of greetings? ....   [1]

(f)   is seeking to explore the widest range of cultures? ....   [1]

(g)   gives an example of how customs can be amusing? ....   [1]

(h)   has least control over where they live? ....   [1]

(i)   talks about cultural differences in their own country? ....   [1]

(j)   knows the most languages? ....   [1]

[Total: 10]

 **Exercise 3**

Read the following article about an ancient custom in an Italian village, and then complete the notes.

THE ITALIAN SNAKE CATCHERS

The serpari (snake catchers) of Cocullo, in Italy, are drinking coffee in the village's only café. Photographs on the walls show famous snakes and snake catchers from the past. Tomorrow is the annual Festival of the Snake Catchers, and one of their responsibilities is to wrap as many snakes as possible around a statue. Then they have the task of carrying the statue through the streets. It is possibly one of the oldest festivals in Europe and certainly one of the strangest.

"If we don't have enough snakes, it will be taken as a bad omen," says Mario, one of the oldest snake catchers. "But I am not too concerned. Lots of people are out searching for snakes at the moment and they will bring them in later today."

The art of snake catching has been passed down from father to son here in Cocullo for thousands of years. When catching snakes, it is acceptable to pin one down with a stick, but a real snake catcher is required to grab them just behind the head with bare hands in a lightning flash of motion. The catchers find the snakes in the rock formations and on the slopes around the village, and the most desired species is the olive-coloured cervone. It loves to climb trees and wrap itself around branches, so it is perfect for staying on the statue of San Domenico during the parade. A large cervone is over two metres long and the man who catches one is a hero for many years to come.

As Mario had predicted, it has been a good day for the snake catchers. They are walking around with snakes in special bags because it is their duty to keep the snakes safe before the festival. The star of the moment, however, is a ten-year-old boy who has caught a large cervone and is now surrounded by a group of people taking selfies.

On the festival day an estimated 30 000 people pour into the village, which has only 250 permanent residents. Photographers are everywhere and all day long there are random bursts of fireworks and explosions from firecrackers. A marching band fights its way through the crowd and queues of hungry people are standing at the many mobile shops that are selling traditional bread and cakes, some shaped like a snake swallowing its tail. There are stalls in the streets selling souvenirs of rubber snakes, wooden snakes and balloon snakes. There are, of course, hundreds of real live snakes and they are all looking for a quiet place to hide. They would prefer to lie on a rock in the sun, far away from here.

With choral music from the sound system, the snake-covered statue is paraded through the crowd. The snake catchers have a duty to pick up fallen snakes and reattach them, because it is a bad omen to have a statue without snakes in the parade. It happened once in the 1980s and the harvest was a disaster that year. The snake catchers also have to ensure that they prevent the snakes from covering the statue's face and eyes… yet another bad omen for the villagers at this unusual festival.

You are going to talk to your local travel club about the Festival of the Snake Catchers.
Prepare some notes as the basis of your talk.

Make short notes under each heading.

Duties of the snake catchers

- ....

- ....

- ....

- ....

- ....

Festival attractions

- ....

- ....

- ....

[Total: 9]

Exercise 4

Read the following article about a Japanese man who has climbed Everest three times. Write a summary about how climbing at extreme heights can affect the body.

Your summary should be about 100 words long (and no more than 120 words long).

You should use your own words as far as possible.

You will receive up to 8 marks for the content of your summary, and up to 8 marks for the style and accuracy of your language.

CLIMBING MOUNT EVEREST AT 80 YEARS OF AGE

Yuichiro Miura, the Japanese adventurer, had already endured three heart operations and extensive surgery to repair a shattered pelvis. He had also battled diabetes. Despite all this, he had twice reached the summit of the world's highest mountain, Everest, once when he was 70 and again at 75-years-old. After a gap of five years, at the age of 80, he attempted to climb it for the third time.

On the first stage of the training for his Everest climb, he strapped weights to his body and legs and walked nine kilometres from a Tokyo station to his office and back every day. In his office he had an altitude training room where he could train in an environment which exactly copied the conditions he would face at 6 000 metres of height. At this altitude, all climbers, whatever their age, experience severe physical changes. The most common is high altitude sickness or vomiting caused by lack of oxygen. In the most extreme cases there can be fluid accumulation in the lungs. In addition, climbers know that a lack of fitness at such heights can lead to symptoms such as hallucinations.

Miura arrived at base camp on Everest and the team began their preparations. The climbers had to start conditioning themselves to the altitude by making several return climbs, reaching higher each time, before attempting the final ascent to the summit. The team was lucky because they had good climbing conditions. If there are severe cold conditions then frostbite can cause vulnerable body parts, such as hands, feet, ears and noses to become black and useless. However, none of the team suffered such problems and, under clear blue skies, they finally reached the summit. Miura said, "When I got there the achievement sank in and I could not believe it. I was standing there for about an hour, I took off my oxygen mask and just enjoyed the view. I was able to make phone calls and let everyone know that we had made it." At above 8 000 metres, a good supply of oxygen is vital because a lack of it can kill a significant number of brain cells. There is also the constant concern about snow blindness because if your eyes are unprotected, the sunlight can burn the cornea, the front part of the eye, causing a sensation like having sand in them.

The body experiences severe physical exhaustion from the climb as a result of constant exercise, lack of oxygen and cold temperatures. Climbers have to drink lots of water and, most importantly, to know their own physical limits.

On Miura's expedition, the really bad weather arrived on the descent and his team just about reached one of the lower camps when a snowstorm started. In such intensely cold and windy conditions, hypothermia can cause a severe drop in body temperature. At the lower camp, Miura's team managed to boil water and eat a high energy cake which gave them the strength to continue down to safety.

Miura says that he is not finished yet. He is now planning to ski down Cho Oyu, the world's sixth highest mountain, when he is 85, and he intends to climb Everest again when he is 90.

....

....

....

....

....

....

....

....

....

....

....

....

....

....

....

....

....

....

....

....

....

[Total: 16]

Self-assessment

Here are some guidelines which you can used to arrive at a mark out of 8 for the **language** that you used in this exercise.

When I finished my written piece I felt...	Yes	No	If yes, ...
Language			
I was confident with my writing and tried very hard to change words and expressions in the text and use my own without making any mistakes. I also concentrated on making the details flow nicely with linking words.			Give yourself 7 or 8 marks.
I made some effort to change words here and there. I thought that my language was correct most of the time.			Give yourself 5 or 6 marks.
I was less confident about changing too many words from the original text and tended to stay with safer, simpler language so that I didn't make mistakes.			Give yourself 3 or 4 marks.
I didn't try to change any words and just simply copied the original. I wasn't able to include any linking words either and I felt that I made mistakes which would have made it hard for the reader to understand what I was trying to say.			Give yourself 2 marks.
I struggled with this exercise and could only copy some detail. I am not sure if the detail was correct or not, and my language had lots of mistakes.			Give yourself 1 mark.

Exercise 5

You have recently finished some part-time work.
Write a letter to a friend about the work.

In your letter you should:

- explain what the job was *and* why you decided to do it;
- describe what you had to do;
- say how you felt after the experience.

Your letter should be between 150 and 200 words long. Do not write an address.

The pictures above may give you some ideas, and you should try to use some ideas of your own.

You will receive up to 8 marks for the content of your letter, and up to 8 marks for the style and accuracy of your language.

....

....

....

....

....

....

....

....

....

....

....

....

....

....

....

....

....

....

....

....

....

....

[Total: 16]

Self-assessment

Two criteria are used to mark this exercise: **content** and **language**, both of which have a maximum mark of 8.

We have converted these into easy-to-use checklists for you.

When I finished my written piece I felt...	Yes	No	If yes, ...
Content			
I developed my ideas very well, writing lots of extra detail. I made sure that I referred to the reader all the time, with a correct formal or informal style. I thought that the reader would find my writing very enjoyable.			Give yourself 8 marks.
I completed all the parts of the task and added some extra ideas and detail. I remembered who I was writing for and wrote in a style that was appropriate.			Give yourself 6 or 7 marks.
My style of writing was OK and I made sure that my piece was always about the subject, but I was not able to add much extra detail.			Give yourself 5 marks.
I wasn't sure that I was successful in keeping to the topic all the time. I didn't have too many ideas and felt that I wrote some things which were not really relevant.			Give yourself 4 marks.
I didn't really think about who was going to read the piece and wrote in the wrong style. I also felt that I was short of ideas and repeated myself at times.			Give yourself 2 or 3 marks.
Language			
I was confident with my writing and used a wide range of very accurate language and even managed to include some good idioms. I made sure that my verb tenses were all correct. All in all, I thought that I made very few errors.			Give yourself 8 marks.
I tried to use some more unusual words and expressions and think that I was generally accurate with them. I remembered to use paragraphs to divide the different ideas that I had.			Give yourself 6 or 7 marks.
I tended to stay with safer, simpler language so that I didn't make mistakes.			Give yourself 4 or 5 marks.
I found the writing hard, made too many mistakes and maybe the person reading my piece would have had problems at times trying to understand it.			Give yourself 2 or 3 marks.

Exercise 6

Your local council recently announced that it plans to hold a major festival in your town. Here are two comments about this idea:

"This will make our town famous!"

"It will cost a lot of money, which could be spent on more important things."

Write a letter to your local council giving your views.

Your letter should be between 150 and 200 words long.

The comments above may give you some ideas, and you should try to use some ideas of your own.

You will receive up to 8 marks for the content of your letter, and up to 8 marks for the style and accuracy of your language.

....

....

....

....

....

....

....

....

....

....

....

....

....

....

....

....

....

....

....

....

....

....

[Total: 16]

Self-assessment

Two criteria are used to mark this exercise: **content** and **language**, both of which have a maximum mark of 8.

We have converted these into easy-to-use checklists for you.

When I finished my written piece I felt...	Yes	No	If yes, ...
Content			
I developed my ideas very well, writing lots of extra detail. I made sure that I referred to the reader all the time, with a correct formal or informal style. I thought that the reader would find my writing very enjoyable.			Give yourself 8 marks.
I completed all the parts of the task and added some extra ideas and detail. I remembered who I was writing for and wrote in a style that was appropriate.			Give yourself 6 or 7 marks.
My style of writing was OK and I made sure that my piece was always about the subject, but I was not able to add much extra detail.			Give yourself 5 marks.
I wasn't sure that I was successful in keeping to the topic all the time. I didn't have too many ideas and felt that I wrote some things which were not really relevant.			Give yourself 4 marks.
I didn't really think about who was going to read the piece and wrote in the wrong style. I also felt that I was short of ideas and repeated myself at times.			Give yourself 2 or 3 marks.
Language			
I was confident with my writing and used a wide range of very accurate language and even managed to include some good idioms. I made sure that my verb tenses were all correct. All in all, I thought that I made very few errors.			Give yourself 8 marks.
I tried to use some more unusual words and expressions and think that I was generally accurate with them. I remembered to use paragraphs to divide the different ideas that I had.			Give yourself 6 or 7 marks.
I tended to stay with safer, simpler language so that I didn't make mistakes.			Give yourself 4 or 5 marks.
I found the writing hard, made too many mistakes and maybe the person reading my piece would have had problems at times trying to understand it.			Give yourself 2 or 3 marks.

Paper 2 Listening

1–4

 Exercise 1

You will hear four short recordings. Answer each question on the line provided. Write no more than **three** words for each answer.

You can play the recording twice.

1 (a) How many job applicants will make it through to Stage 2?

.... [1]

(b) What is different about Stage 2 compared to Stage 1?

.... [1]

2 (a) What was the temperature in the morning?

.... [1]

(b) How much snow fell in total?

.... [1]

3 (a) What is the employee's employment number?

.... [1]

(b) What will he have to provide after three days of illness?

.... [1]

4 (a) What did the owner think was wrong with her cat?

.... [1]

(b) What does the vet suggest that the owner does to help the cat?

.... [1]

[Total: 8]

Exercise 2

5   You will hear a talk given by a judge, describing her career and her experiences. Listen to the talk and complete the notes below. Write **one** or **two** words only or a **number** in each gap.

You can play the recording twice.

Shoukara's early life

Graduated from university with a .... in Canada

Parents were living in Canada due to their work

Shoukara moved to her current home when she was ....

Shoukara's early career

Preferred criminal rights law due to the lack of .... in society

Joined a law firm called *Free the World*

Worked mostly as a .... lawyer

Recollections about being a judge

Was 52 when appointed as a judge

Main qualities needed were speaking less and ....

Lived in special quarters during a case

Was told not to discuss her work when she was at home

Was once driven around in a .... vehicle

Favourite court was number 4 because it is the oldest

Court 4 has 80 figures of previous High Court judges and a gold desk

The problem with Court 4 was that it was ....

The purpose of her talk

To focus on three interesting cases:

1) her most challenging one

2) the case which attracted the ....

3) the case which she found the funniest

[Total: 8]

Exercise 3

6 You will hear six people talking about their views on work and their own careers. For each of Speakers 1 to 6, choose from the list, **A** to **G**, which opinion each speaker expresses.

Write the letter in the box. Use each letter only once. There is one extra letter which you do not need to use.

Speaker 1 _____

Speaker 2 _____

Speaker 3 _____

Speaker 4 _____

Speaker 5 _____

Speaker 6 _____

A It's never a good idea to rush into a job as you may end up following the wrong career.

B Manual labour is important in people's everyday lives.

C It's better to plan a career, and from as young an age as you can.

D You will never find a job that is perfect, so do your best to enjoy the good days!

E You shouldn't take a job too seriously. It's really important to be able to tell some jokes at work and be humorous.

F To be able to manage your own workload is the most important factor.

G Work is a means to an end. It's all about earning money and that's the main motivation.

[Total: 6]

Exercise 4

7 You will hear Somchai talking about the Tiger Kingdom in Thailand, where he works. Listen to the conversation and look at the questions. For each question choose the correct answer, **A**, **B** or **C**, and put a tick (✓) in the appropriate box.

You can play the talk twice.

(a) In the hot season, tigers

    A are not cold. ☐

    B seem more lazy. ☐

    C lie down and move less. ☐ [1]

(b) The tigers bond with the handlers as a result of

    A patience, freedom and repeated tasks. ☐

    B building trust by taking time and repeating tasks. ☐

    C repeating tasks and bonding with each other. ☐ [1]

(c) When stroking a tiger

    A be careful. ☐

    B be gentle. ☐

    C be firm. ☐ [1]

(d) The Tiger Kingdom has an age policy in which

    A adults can spend time with all tigers. ☐

    B older teenagers can spend time with older tigers. ☐

    C young children can spend time with young tigers. ☐ [1]

(e) It is natural for a tiger to

    A sleep more in the cold weather. ☐

    B sleep for much of the day. ☐

    C want to be very lively. ☐ [1]

(f)   Where are tigers officially endangered?

     A   Only in parts of Asia. ☐

     B   Mainly in Vietnam. ☐

     C   Everywhere. ☐   [1]

(g)   Tiger Kingdom plays a role in tiger conservation by

     A   producing lots of tiger cubs. ☐

     B   stopping all species of tiger from becoming extinct. ☐

     C   being home to six breeding pairs of Indo Chinese tigers. ☐   [1]

(h)   The Tiger Kingdom organisation has

     A   grown steadily to 212 tigers in three compounds. ☐

     B   grown very slowly to 212 tigers and two restaurants. ☐

     C   grown carefully to 212 tigers, two restaurants and two branches. ☐   [1]

[Total: 8]

Exercise 5

8(a) You will hear a man, called Jorgen, talking to the media prior to the opening of the Berlin Festival of Light, which is an annual event in Berlin, Germany. Listen to the talk and complete the notes in Part A. Write one or two words only in each gap.

You can play the talk twice.

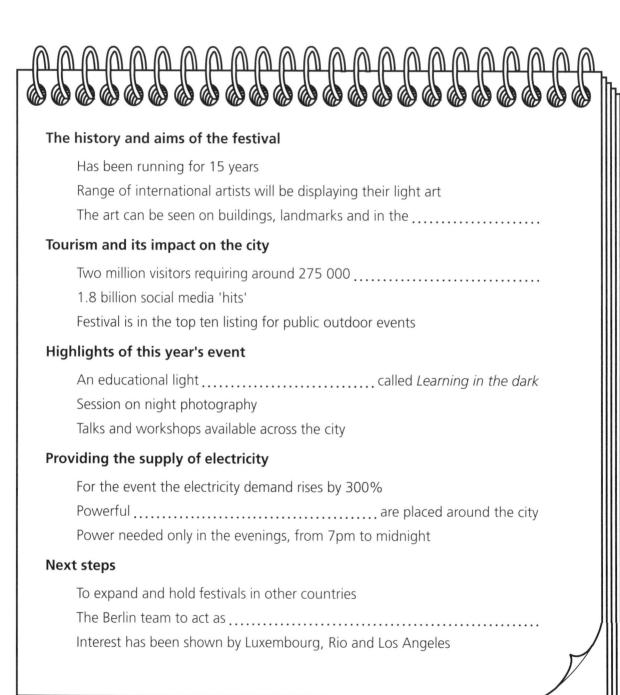

The history and aims of the festival

Has been running for 15 years

Range of international artists will be displaying their light art

The art can be seen on buildings, landmarks and in the ....

Tourism and its impact on the city

Two million visitors requiring around 275 000 ....

1.8 billion social media 'hits'

Festival is in the top ten listing for public outdoor events

Highlights of this year's event

An educational light .... called *Learning in the dark*

Session on night photography

Talks and workshops available across the city

Providing the supply of electricity

For the event the electricity demand rises by 300%

Powerful .... are placed around the city

Power needed only in the evenings, from 7pm to midnight

Next steps

To expand and hold festivals in other countries

The Berlin team to act as ....

Interest has been shown by Luxembourg, Rio and Los Angeles

[Total: 5]

Exercise 5

8(b) Now listen to a conversation between two trainee journalists, who have been listening to the talk given to the media about the festival. Complete the sentences in Part B. Write one or two words only in each gap.

You can play the conversation twice.

Writing an article about the Berlin Festival of Light

(a) It is the .... time Heidi has written about the festival.

(b) The multi-coloured face display features .... faces.

(c) Video mapping is popular with ....

(d) The two journalists would like to see the festival reach .... in the top ten list.

(e) Heidi is keen to learn more about using light art in ....

[Total: 5]

Paper 3 Speaking

 ### GETTING OUTDOORS

More and more people across the world are entertaining themselves indoors, and in many cases by using their smartphones and tablets. What about getting outdoors more? Discuss this topic with the examiner.

Use the following five prompts, in the order given below, to develop the conversation:

- how much time you spend indoors and outdoors
- some people you know who you feel ought to get outdoors more
- the challenges of getting outdoors where you live and in general across the world
- the suggestion that people who do spend more time outdoors are healthier; both in body and in mind
- the idea that governments should get rid of all border controls and passports, so that we can all just go wherever we want to.

You may introduce related ideas of your own to expand on these prompts.

Remember, you are not allowed to make any written notes.

[Total: 30]

Self-assessment

In the speaking test there are three criteria which are used to arrive at a mark out of 30 for your performance in the test as a whole.

We have converted these into easy-to-use checklists for you.

My performance	Yes	No	If yes, …
Structure			
I used a wide range of accurate sentences and phrases, and felt confident all the way through.			Give yourself 9 or 10 marks.
I felt competent throughout and only struggled a little when I tried to be too complex.			Give yourself 7 or 8 marks.
I tended to stay with safer, simpler language so as not to make any mistakes.			Give yourself 5 or 6 marks.
I struggled and made too many mistakes in my spoken language.			Give yourself 3 or 4 marks.
Vocabulary			
I used a sophisticated range of words and used them at the right times.			Give yourself 9 or 10 marks.
I used a wide range of words and felt that it was sufficient to ensure a competent discussion.			Give yourself 7 or 8 marks.
I used an adequate range of words, but stumbled a little and used the wrong words at times.			Give yourself 5 or 6 marks.
I struggled more and hesitated to find the right words. I felt my vocabulary was limited.			Give yourself 3 or 4 marks.
Development and fluency			
I responded to all prompts confidently and felt that I spoke very clearly and naturally.			Give yourself 9 or 10 marks.
I responded to most prompts and only needed a little help at times.			Give yourself 7 or 8 marks.
I felt that the discussion was a partial success, but that I could have contributed more.			Give yourself 5 or 6 marks.
I struggled and gave too many short responses. I felt that the discussion was not successful and I struggled also to speak naturally and clearly.			Give yourself 3 or 4 marks.

Now add up your marks to arrive at a mark out of 30.

If your total mark is in the range:

- 25–30: you are doing really well
- 20–24: this is fine, but more practice is likely to help you a lot
- 15–19: it's a safe and secure performance
- 9–14: you are struggling a little and you should practise as much as you can by listening to lots of recorded discussions and taking part in as many discussions as you can. Start with shorter ones and gradually develop them.

Further practice

Paper 1 Reading and writing

 **Exercise 1**

Read the following article about Uluru/Ayers Rock in Australia, and then answer the questions.

THE CULTURAL HEART OF AUSTRALIA

Uluru/Ayers Rock is an enormous sandstone rock formation in Central Australia and is situated 450 kilometres by road from the nearest town, Alice Springs. It is 348 metres high with a circumference of 9.4 kilometres and it takes about three hours to complete the walk around the whole rock. It is one of Australia's most recognisable natural landmarks and the best way to see Uluru/Ayers Rock is to go on a guided hike because you can then get a true idea of just how big it is.

The rock is particularly famous for appearing to change colour at different times of the day and year, especially when it glows red at dawn and sunset. One of the most enjoyable things to do there is to have a sunset dinner with the rock forming a majestic background. At other times of the day, the colour shades change from black to orange, finally becoming a deep crimson.

The rock has a double name because it contains both the traditional Aboriginal and the more recent English name. It has great cultural significance for the Anangu people, the traditional inhabitants of the area, who nowadays lead walking tours to inform visitors about the local flora and fauna and retell the Aboriginal Dreamtime stories of their culture. Countless legends surround this rock. Every crack and cave tells a story from the Dreamtime, the name given to the time of creation by the indigenous Anangu people. In one story there was a great battle between Kuniya, the young python snakeboy, and the evil snake, Liru. Spears flew high in the air and one killed Kuniya. According to the story, the deep holes which are across the south face of the rock are where the spears landed.

The development of tourist facilities near to the base of the rock began in the 1950s and soon had a negative impact on the surrounding environment. The park is now listed as a World Heritage Site and increased tourism has brought economic benefits to the Anangu people and the region. There is, however, a real challenge to try and keep their original cultural values and at the same time meet the needs of tourists. The rock remains the cultural heart of Australia, but tourism here has been very controversial since the beginning. In the early days, tourists were encouraged to visit the rock and take the opportunity to climb it. There are now many people who want the climbing to be banned, but this activity would need to be replaced with other attractions to avoid a drop in visitor numbers. The local Anangu people do not climb the rock because of its great cultural significance and would prefer visitors not to climb it out of respect for their laws and culture. Moreover, many people say that there are already many other different ways to experience the majesty of the rock, and a gentle camel trek is one of the most popular. Alternatively, hiring a cycle to explore a wider area around the rock is strongly encouraged because of its minimal damage to the environment.

(a) How many kilometres is it to go around Uluru/Ayers Rock?

.... [1]

(b) What does the rock look like at the beginning and the end of the day?

.... [1]

(c) Why does the rock have two names?

.... [1]

(d) How do the Anangu people help tourists? Give **two** details.

....

.... [2]

(e) What evidence on the rock is there of a battle?

.... [1]

(f) What caused damage to the environment close to the rock?

.... [1]

(g) What is the great difficulty that the Anangu people face nowadays?

.... [1]

(h) What is one possible consequence of stopping people climbing the rock?

.... [1]

(i) What activities are now recommended when visiting Uluru/Ayers Rock? Give **four** details.

....

....

....

.... [4]

[Total: 13]

Exercise 2

Read the article about four people (**A–D**) who present their views about food. Then answer Question **10 (a)–(j)**.

FOOD GLORIOUS FOOD!

Four people contribute to a monthly magazine about food. The magazine covers cooking food at home but also eating out at restaurants.

A I have had my noodle shop for nearly 10 years now. It's always very busy but that's the way I like it. Most of our customers come here for lunch but as we're open from 10 in the morning until 3 in the afternoon, this can be a very long lunchtime for me and my staff. We only serve four different types of noodles, so it's easy for us to maintain a high standard, as we don't experiment very much with the menu. Our customers choose the type of noodle they want to eat, and then they add the meat, and the various sauces we offer. I thoroughly enjoy my noodle shop. We get quite a range of people coming in to eat lunch from millionaires, to shop workers, to students, and sometimes we get the local police force coming in. It's amazing how the simple dish of noodles can bring these people, from very different walks of life, together in one place, creating a vibrant atmosphere.

B I have been a vegetarian for the last 15 years, ever since I was 18 years old. I am 33 years old now and I enjoy being a vegetarian. I don't eat meat for two reasons. Firstly, I don't think humans need to eat meat and I believe in protecting animals and not eating them, and secondly, I feel much healthier by not eating meat or meat products. It is much easier nowadays to find vegetarian food in shops and supermarkets, and to eat out at vegetarian restaurants. One thing I enjoy is planning my holidays around the wonderful vegetarian festivals that many cities have each year. I prefer to holiday in cities anyway, so seeing city life and being part of a vegetarian week is perfect for me. I have lots of friends who are meat eaters, and they argue that humans need meat to get protein and certain enzymes - so we have an ongoing debate about that. It's all good-natured though – we all remain friends!

C I'd like to tell you how much my eating habits have changed since I became a mother. I have a young child who has just turned one year old, and I didn't realise how much having children would change my diet. By profession, I am a manager of several retail stores, and my job means I travel a lot and stay in nice hotels and eat at lovely restaurants. My clients like to impress me, and quite often they will take me to some very expensive restaurants. You could say that I have become used to eating cuisine of a high standard. But all that has changed since I took a year off work to spend time with my daughter. She eats basic food of course, and now that she is a one year old, she needs to eat proper food and not baby food. I find myself cooking very simple food so that we can share it. It's a long way away from the 5-star treatment I have been used to, but I suppose it is healthier.

D As an Olympic athlete, I have a very specialised diet. I am a middle-distance runner; my best distance is 1500 metres, and as such I need a diet which gives me carbohydrate, and proteins to build my muscles. My diet is very regular, which means that I eat pretty much the same food each day. My breakfast is always cereals and fruit, and my lunch is always rice and meat (lean meat of course). For dinner, I tend to eat pasta as that gives me a slow release of energy which stops me getting hungry, until I eat breakfast again. I never have any snacks, and I avoid high fat food. I take in a lot of liquids – probably 4 to 6 litres a day of water or sugar-free drinks. Most people I meet think my food must be very boring, but I feel that the opposite is true. I have learned to appreciate food in a way that some other people don't. I don't take food for granted, and I never eat too much, as I cannot afford to get overweight and unfit. After all, we are what we eat!

The questions below are about the people (A–D) who send letters to a magazine about food.

For each question write the correct letter A, B, C or D on the line.

Which person …

(a) feels that food can create a single, lively community? .... [1]

(b) pays the closest attention to their diet? .... [1]

(c) realises that their diet has improved with recent life changes? .... [1]

(d) eats food based on strong personal views? .... [1]

(e) believes that water is as important as food? .... [1]

(f) stays with the same tried and trusted food? .... [1]

(g) probably eats the highest quality food? .... [1]

(h) has made the biggest change to their diet? .... [1]

(i) discusses eating habits the most? .... [1]

(j) connects holidays with food? .... [1]

[Total: 10]

 **Exercise 3**

Read the following article about people who run with bulls through the streets of Pamplona, Spain, and then complete the notes.

RUNNING WITH THE BULLS

During the annual festival of San Fermin in Pamplona, Spain, there is the famous event of the running of the bulls. Many daring people run with a group of six bulls that have been let loose on a course through the town's streets.

According to Spanish tradition, the true origin of the run began in the 14th century. While transporting cattle to the market, men would try to speed-up the process by hurrying their cattle using tactics of fear and excitement. Over the years it turned into a competition, as young adults would attempt to race in front of the bulls and make it safely to the bulls' enclosure. The popularity of this practice increased and the tradition exists to this day.

At the start of the run, the first rocket is set off at 8am to alert the runners that the gate to the enclosure containing the bulls has been opened. A second rocket then signals that all six bulls have been released and the excitement begins. The bulls, running at an average speed of 20 kilometres per hour, quickly close up to the runners. Some of the runners stay ahead of the bulls for seconds, others fall and try to avoid the animals, while others press themselves against the walls of the houses in the street hoping that the bulls will race past them. So it continues for 875 metres to the end of the course with the average time to complete the run being two minutes and 30 seconds.

The event is loved by the Spanish generally and they are the main nationality taking part with some people returning to it year-after-year. The Spanish traditions are closely observed and an outsider has to adapt to them, but running with the bulls is growing in popularity as an extreme sport among foreigners. The runners are traditionally dressed in white shirts and trousers with a red sash tied around the middle and a red scarf around their neck. This is an event adored by brave young men, who love the danger and excitement of the situation. There is a large amount of media coverage for the event, many television and radio reporters are there to film the event and interview the main characters. Many writers and photographers are enthusiastic about the running of the bulls because it gives them the chance to film and write about this exciting event. One writer from Canada says that he sees the festival as a chance to make new friends and to renew old acquaintances.

There can be problems if the bulls do not stay together and decide to separate, and every year between 50 and 100 people are injured during the run. In order to minimise the impact of injuries, 200 volunteers and Red Cross workers are ready to give medical attention. There is a first-aid post every 50 metres on average, each one with at least a doctor and a nurse in attendance. In addition to these posts, there are about 20 ambulances which makes it possible to have an injured person taken to hospital in less than 10 minutes.

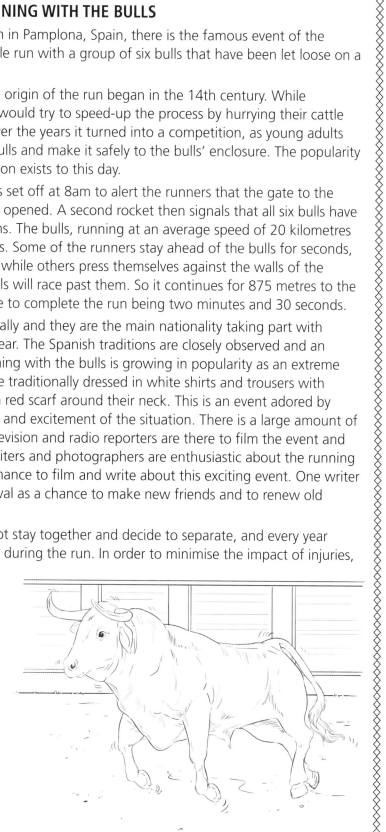

There are always some serious injuries during the event, but most of those who take part in the run would consider that a small price to pay for such an adrenaline rush.

You are going to talk to your school geography society about the bull-running festival in Pamplona. Prepare some notes as the basis of your talk.

Make your notes under each heading.

Facts about times and distances of the bull run

- ....

- ....

- ....

Who the bull run is popular with

- ....

- ....

- ....

Details of medical support

- ....

- ....

- ....

[Total: 9]

 **Exercise 4**

Read the following article about places around the world which are 'twinned' or linked with each other.

Write a summary about the reasons for twinning and why some people would like to stop it.

Your summary should be about 100 words long (and no more than 120 words long).

You should use your own words as far as possible.

You will receive up to 8 marks for the content of your summary, and up to 8 marks for the style and accuracy of your language.

TWINNING AROUND THE WORLD

When towns, cities or maybe even countries are 'twinned', it can be described as a kind of agreement between each other. Maybe the town where you live has a sign at the entrance with some words on it which say 'Twinned with…' and it tells you the name of the place and the country. Have you ever wondered what this place in another country is like? Maybe you have visited it with your school or local club and met the people there and had a good time.

Why do we have twinning anyway? The original reason for twinning was to promote friendship and understanding between different countries. One European schoolteacher, who takes her students on a trip to the USA every two years, says, "From these visits, the students get a huge amount of experience of a totally different culture which they learn a lot about by taking part in musical performances, art exhibitions and cultural festivals."

One purpose of the twinning arrangements is to encourage trade and it has been increasingly used to form business links between towns and cities. For example, one French ice-cream company recently opened a factory in Eastern Europe and although business is not the main purpose of twinning, these relationships are a natural development of partner town links.

How do towns and cities select a possible partner? One interesting example was in 2012 when the village of Dull, in Scotland, and the American town of Boring, in the state of Oregon, agreed to twin to promote tourism and used their unusual names to good effect. It seems that geographical distance has very little influence on the choice of a partner town. In fact, the further apart the places are the greater the differences in lifestyle, which means that there are more interesting things to learn about each other. One other important aspect of twinning is to learn a new language and many students have been helped to improve their linguistic skills by direct contact with foreign students and their families.

There are others who hold the opinion that such links do not have any purpose in the 21st century. Some towns are starting to abandon their twinning partnerships because they do not see the arrangement as being relevant in today's society. They say that world travel has become widely available and communication links have improved. With Skype and the Internet, it is not necessary to have groups of people travelling distances to other regions and we should make better use of information technology to keep in contact. They argue that in these days of economic difficulty it is hard to justify the spending of money on such projects, even if the twin town or city is close and the visits do not cost very much. People travel so much more that the idea of fixing on one place is inconsistent with the free movement that many of us expect nowadays.

It is a strange situation that as the world gets smaller through easier travel and faster communications, so friendship links with countries of different cultures and traditions are becoming more difficult to maintain.

....

....

....

....

....

....

....

....

....

....

....

....

....

....

....

....

....

....

....

....

....

[Total: 16]

Self-assessment

Here are some guidelines which you can used to arrive at a mark out of 8 for the **language** that you used in this exercise.

When I finished my written piece I felt...	Yes	No	If yes, ...
I was confident with my writing and tried very hard to change words and expressions in the text and use my own without making any mistakes. I also concentrated on making the details flow nicely with linking words.			Give yourself 7 or 8 marks.
I made some effort to change words here and there. I thought that my language was correct most of the time.			Give yourself 5 or 6 marks.
I was less confident about changing too many words from the original text and tended to stay with safer, simpler language so that I didn't make mistakes.			Give yourself 3 or 4 marks.
I didn't try to change any words and just simply copied the original. I wasn't able to include any linking words either and I felt that I made mistakes which would have made it hard for the reader to understand what I was trying to say.			Give yourself 2 marks.
I struggled with this exercise and could only copy some detail. I am not sure if the detail was correct or not, and my language had lots of mistakes.			Give yourself 1 mark.

Exercise 5

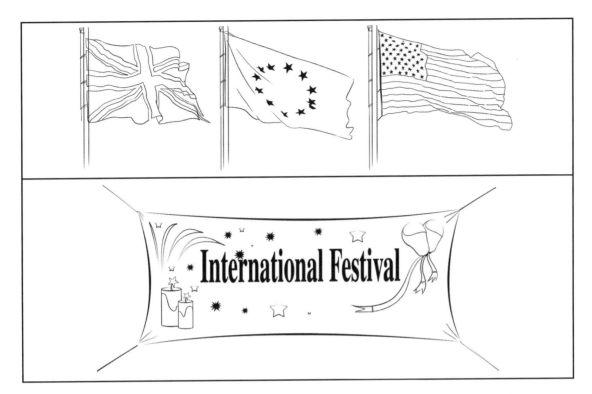

You have just helped to organise a special school day to celebrate one of your country's traditions.

Write an email to a friend about the festival.

In your email you should:

- explain why you were organising the special day;
- describe the main event of the day;
- say why you think the day was or was not a success.

Your email should be between 150 and 200 words long. Do not write an address.

The pictures above may give you some ideas, and you should try to use some ideas of your own.

You will receive up to 8 marks for the content of your email, and up to 8 marks for the style and accuracy of your language.

....

....

....

....

....

....

....

....

....

....

....

....

....

....

....

....

....

....

....

....

....

[Total: 16]

Self-assessment

Two criteria are used to mark this exercise: **content** and **language**, both of which have a maximum mark of 8.

We have converted these into easy-to-use checklists for you.

When I finished my written piece I felt...	Yes	No	If yes, ...
Content			
I developed my ideas very well, writing lots of extra detail. I made sure that I referred to the reader all the time, with a correct formal or informal style. I thought that the reader would find my writing very enjoyable.			Give yourself 8 marks.
I completed all the parts of the task and added some extra ideas and detail. I remembered who I was writing for and wrote in a style that was appropriate.			Give yourself 6 or 7 marks.
My style of writing was OK and I made sure that my piece was always about the subject, but I was not able to add much extra detail.			Give yourself 5 marks.
I wasn't sure that I was successful in keeping to the topic all the time. I didn't have too many ideas and felt that I wrote some things which were not really relevant.			Give yourself 4 marks.
I didn't really think about who was going to read the piece and wrote in the wrong style. I also felt that I was short of ideas and repeated myself at times.			Give yourself 2 or 3 marks.
Language			
I was confident with my writing and used a wide range of very accurate language and even managed to include some good idioms. I made sure that my verb tenses were all correct. All in all, I thought that I made very few errors.			Give yourself 8 marks.
I tried to use some more unusual words and expressions and think that I was generally accurate with them. I remembered to use paragraphs to divide the different ideas that I had.			Give yourself 6 or 7 marks.
I tended to stay with safer, simpler language so that I didn't make mistakes.			Give yourself 4 or 5 marks.
I found the writing hard, made too many mistakes and maybe the person reading my piece would have had problems at times trying to understand it.			Give yourself 2 or 3 marks.

Exercise 6

Some people think our planet needs to produce more and more food and using chemicals is the best way to do it.

Here are two comments about this idea:

"I'm worried that chemicals are bad for our health."

"This is the best way to feed the world."

Write an article for your school magazine giving your views about this issue.

Your article should be between 150 and 200 words long.

The comments above may give you some ideas, and you should try to use some ideas of your own.

You will receive up to 8 marks for the content of your article, and up to 8 marks for the style and accuracy of your language.

....

....

....

....

....

....

....

....

....

....

....

....

....

....

....

....

....

....

....

....

....

....

....

....

[Total: 16]

Self-assessment

Two criteria are used to mark this exercise: **content** and **language**, both of which have a maximum mark of 8.

We have converted these into easy-to-use checklists for you.

When I finished my written piece I felt...	Yes	No	If yes, ...
Content			
I developed my ideas very well, writing lots of extra detail. I made sure that I referred to the reader all the time, with a correct formal or informal style. I thought that the reader would find my writing very enjoyable.			Give yourself 8 marks.
I completed all the parts of the task and added some extra ideas and detail. I remembered who I was writing for and wrote in a style that was appropriate.			Give yourself 6 or 7 marks.
My style of writing was OK and I made sure that my piece was always about the subject, but I was not able to add much extra detail.			Give yourself 5 marks.
I wasn't sure that I was successful in keeping to the topic all the time. I didn't have too many ideas and felt that I wrote some things which were not really relevant.			Give yourself 4 marks.
I didn't really think about who was going to read the piece and wrote in the wrong style. I also felt that I was short of ideas and repeated myself at times.			Give yourself 2 or 3 marks.
Language			
I was confident with my writing and used a wide range of very accurate language and even managed to include some good idioms. I made sure that my verb tenses were all correct. All in all, I thought that I made very few errors.			Give yourself 8 marks.
I tried to use some more unusual words and expressions and think that I was generally accurate with them. I remembered to use paragraphs to divide the different ideas that I had.			Give yourself 6 or 7 marks.
I tended to stay with safer, simpler language so that I didn't make mistakes.			Give yourself 4 or 5 marks.
I found the writing hard, made too many mistakes and maybe the person reading my piece would have had problems at times trying to understand it.			Give yourself 2 or 3 marks.

Paper 2 Listening

 Exercise 1

You will hear four short recordings. Answer each question on the line provided. Write no more than **three** words for each answer.

You can play each recording twice.

1 (a) Why does Andrea say she prefers this particular bank?

.... [1]

(b) What type of bank account will she open?

.... [1]

2 (a) How much of the ice cap in the South Pole is melting away each year?

.... [1]

(b) What does the speaker want the people in the audience to do?

.... [1]

3 (a) What is Ahmed's friend tired of being reminded of?

.... [1]

(b) What does Ahmed feel we can all learn from his history lesson?

.... [1]

4 (a) How many islands can a tourist enjoy while visiting Hawaii?

.... [1]

(b) Where do Hawaiian people seem to enjoy holding their parties?

.... [1]

[Total: 8]

ans 160
165

Exercise 2

5 You will hear a talk given by a senior member of the Navajo governing council in the United States of America. Listen to the talk and complete the notes below. Write **one** or **two** words only or a **number** in each gap.
You can play the recording twice.

The Navajo nation

  The word 'Yazzie' means ....

  Navajo land covers around .... miles

  Geographical area is larger than 10 of the 50 states

The Navajo language

  Used to come up with a .... during the war

  Current government conducts some of its duties using Navajo language

The Navajo economy

  Needs to support a population of a quarter of a million people

  Finding .... about a hundred years ago created early wealth

  In 1923 a tribal government was established

  Most sophisticated form of American Indian government

  The Navajo council has 88 members serving .... separate communities

The Navajo government buildings

  The chambers feature vivid .... showing aspects of history

  An organised tour can be arranged via main office in Arizona

The Navajo Times newspaper

  Provided .... to the Navajo people

  Features story about success of the women's wrestling team

  Features a new education project with a nearby university

  All Star Awards Ceremony taking place at ....

[Total: 8]

🔊 Exercise 3

6 You will hear six people talking about global issues and the way forward for the people of planet Earth. For each of Speakers 1 to 6, choose from the list, **A** to **G**, which opinion each speaker expresses. Write the letter in the box. Use each letter only once. There is one extra letter which you do not need to use.

Speaker 1 ____

Speaker 2 ____

Speaker 3 ____

Speaker 4 ____

Speaker 5 ____

Speaker 6 ____

A When providing help, the emphasis should be on a wide range of support systems.

B It's as if we need to start again, and then we might see a new way of living together harmoniously.

C The best way forward is for one nation to take the lead and insist on being tolerant to all other nations around the world.

D Let's address issues in our own country first.

E The future looks bleak and if anything we will become less global in our outlook.

F It is the duty of a more prosperous country to help those less fortunate.

G A true global world will emerge, but only if people are given the chance to engage fully with other people.

[Total: 6]

Exercise 4

7 You will hear Jane talking about what she feels we can learn from the past and her approach to history. Listen to the conversation and look at the questions. For each question choose the correct answer, **A**, **B** or **C**, and put a tick (✓) in the appropriate box.
You can play the talk twice.

(a) Books about the past are

    A the only useful documents. ☐

    B useful, along with other resources. ☐

    C reliable and usually accurate. ☐ [1]

(b) Jane says it is important to also look at

    A art, oral stories and books from older cultures. ☐

    B oral stories, art and older films. ☐

    C wall paintings, films and written drafts of oral stories. ☐ [1]

(c) Jane's new book uses a multi-media approach to

    A allow the reader to navigate how he or she wants to. ☐

    B reduce the impact of traditional history writing. ☐

    C sell more copies as it is interactive. ☐ [1]

(d) Jane is interested in

    A facts more than people. ☐

    B people as much as facts. ☐

    C facts, but not as much as people. ☐ [1]

(e) Historians can be compared to detectives because they

    A usually come up with an objective truth which cannot be challenged. ☐

    B both operate in the same way when they are working. ☐

    C are happy to make the wrong decisions along the way. ☐ [1]

(f) Doctoring is

    A reinventing history. ☐

    B revisiting history. ☐

    C reliving history. ☐ [1]

(g) It is fair to say that Jane sees history repeating itself

    A as unavoidable. ☐

    B as unpredictable. ☐

    C as avoidable. ☐ [1]

(h) People who lived in the past

    A were probably quite different to people today. ☐

    B lived in a similar way to how most people live today. ☐

    C could not lead ordinary lives due to how they had to live to survive. ☐ [1]

[Total: 8]

Exercise 5

8 (a) You will hear a woman, called Juliette, talking about the self-sufficient community she lives among in the south of France. Listen to the talk and complete the notes in Part A. Write one or two words only in each gap.

You can play the talk twice.

The location of the community

A hilly region in the south of France

Temperate climate and ....

The farm

Is about 250 acres in size

Requires about .... to run efficiently

Does not make a profit

Aims to show that self-sufficiency can help the wider community

The goat herd

Goats are cunning and agile

The goats escaped and ate ....

Juliette learned that animals don't always eat sensibly

Other challenges faced

Lost a potato crop due to blight

Having to repair worn-out plumbing

Maintaining the .... as they are old

Volunteers

Find out about the farm on the Internet

Join for .... only

Provide unpaid work in exchange for an experience

[Total: 5]

 **Exercise 5**

8 (b) Now listen to a conversation between two young teenagers in the audience who have been listening to the talk given by Juliette, about the self-sufficient community farm. Complete the sentences in Part B. Write one or two words only in each gap.

You can play the conversation twice.

Life on the farm

(a) Leela is reconsidering because she doesn't want to work on .... plumbing and machines.

(b) The experience has encouraged Demetri to think about a .... in agriculture.

(c) Demetri's hobby is to fix ....

Self-sufficiency

(d) Leela has decided that she would prefer .... life.

(e) They both feel that the self-sufficiency groups in California are ....

[Total: 5]

Paper 3 Speaking

CULTURE AND COMMUNITY

Global issues are important for us all, but of equal importance to many are issues closer to home. Discuss this topic with the examiner.

Use the following five prompts, in the order given below, to develop the conversation:

- the area, region and the culture in which you live
- some local and regional issues that you, or people you know have identified as concerns
- the pros and cons of a multi-cultural community
- the suggestion that local or regional matters should be prioritised over global matters
- the view that there is no such thing as a global community.

You may introduce related ideas of your own to expand on these prompts.

Remember, you are not allowed to make any written notes.

[Total: 30]

Self-assessment

In the speaking test there are three criteria which are used to arrive at a mark out of 30 for your performance in the test as a whole.

We have converted these into easy-to-use checklists for you.

My performance	Yes	No	If yes, …
Structure			
I used a wide range of accurate sentences and phrases, and felt confident all the way through.	8		Give yourself 9 or 10 marks.
I felt competent throughout and only struggled a little when I tried to be too complex.	6		Give yourself 7 or 8 marks.
I tended to stay with safer, simpler language so not to make any mistakes.	6		Give yourself 5 or 6 marks.
I struggled and made too many mistakes in my spoken language.	4		Give yourself 3 or 4 marks.
Vocabulary			
I used a sophisticated range of words and used them at the right times.	9		Give yourself 9 or 10 marks.
I used a wide range of words and felt that it was sufficient to ensure a competent discussion.	7		Give yourself 7 or 8 marks.
I used an adequate range of words, but stumbled a little and used the wrong words at times.	6		Give yourself 5 or 6 marks.
I struggled more and hesitated to find the right words. I felt my vocabulary was limited.	4		Give yourself 3 or 4 marks.
Development and fluency			
I responded to all prompts confidently and felt that I spoke very clearly and naturally.	9		Give yourself 9 or 10 marks.
I responded to most prompts and only needed a little help at times.	8		Give yourself 7 or 8 marks.
I felt that the discussion was a partial success, but that I could have contributed more.	6		Give yourself 5 or 6 marks.
I struggled and gave too many short responses. I felt that the discussion was not successful and I struggled also to speak naturally and clearly.	4		Give yourself 3 or 4 marks.

By adding up your marks, you will arrive at a mark out of 30.

If your total mark is in the range:

- 25–30: you are doing really well
- 20–24: this is fine, but more practice is likely to help you a lot
- 15–19: it's a safe and secure performance
- 9–14: you are struggling a little and you should practise as much as you can by listening to lots of recorded discussions and taking part in as many discussions as you can. Start with shorter ones and gradually develop them.

Mark scheme

Paper 1: Reading and writing

Exercise 1

Question	Answer	Marks
a	French	[1]
b	while he was at school	[1]
c	<u>first</u> decided to experiment with aircraft design	[1]
d	climbed out of his seat AND threw himself towards the tail **(BOTH DETAILS REQUIRED FOR TWO MARKS.)**	[2]
e	1908 passed with no serious attempt to fly across the Channel	[1]
f	one of the windiest periods of the summer	[1]
g	possibility of one <u>brief</u> moment of better weather	[1]
h	followed the ship guiding him towards Dover	[1]
i	1904 first person to fly for more than five minutes 1908 newspaper offered £500 prize money 1909 first cross-Channel flight 1927 first cross-Atlantic flight 1930s start to develop jet engines **(ANY FOUR FROM THE ABOVE, ONE MARK EACH.)**	[4]

[Total: 13]

Exercise 2

Question	Answer	Marks
a	A	[1]
b	B	[1]
c	C	[1]
d	C	[1]
e	B	[1]
f	D	[1]
g	A	[1]
h	B	[1]
i	D	[1]
j	B	[1]

[Total: 10]

Exercise 3

Here are some points to include, which could earn you up to 9 marks.

Heading	Answer	Marks
Description of the camp	(a) large circle of tents	[1]
	(b) camp fire	[1]
	(c) toilet block	[1]
	(d) no showers	[1]
Any three from the above. Maximum for this section 3		
Philosophy of the organisers	(e) explore literature in a new way	[1]
	(f) allow children to find their own adventures	[1]
	(g) independent thought / independent behaviour essential when growing up	[1]
	(h) children show due care and respect	[1]
	(i) books are not a solitary experience	[1]
Any four from the above. Maximum for this section 4		
Daily tasks of the teenagers in the camp	(j) collect wood	[1]
	(k) light fires	[1]
	(l) clean and tidy central area	[1]
Any two from the above. Maximum for this section 2		

[Total: 9]

Exercise 4

Content

Here are some points to include about the content, which could earn you up to 8 marks.

Point	Content answer	Marks
1	automated transport / single digital ticket	[1]
2	commuting to work safer / traffic accidents reduced	[1]
3	machine learning / talk to artificially intelligent 'personal assistants'	[1]
4	medical supply deliveries	[1]
5	carry out precision surgical operations	[1]
6	automated porters in hospitals	[1]
7	robot cleaners	[1]
8	companion robots for the elderly	[1]

[Total: 8]

Language

You can also get up to 8 marks for language. Use the self-assessment checklist to check your progress. If you can, show your work to your teacher.

Exercises 5 and 6: For exercises 5 and 6, you will be awarded a mark out of 16. Use the self-assessment grids to mark your answers. If you can, show your work to your teacher.

Paper 2: Listening

Exercise 1

Question	Answer	Marks
1a	carry passengers	[1]
1b	*under* 4 hours	[1]
2a	1829	[1]
2b	nuclear unit	[1]
3a	Dr Roberts / the second one / Tuesday at 5pm **(All of these would be acceptable as long as no more than three words are used and the spelling of *Roberts* is close enough. 'Dr Roberts at 5pm' should not be allowed as it is four words and not all of that detail is needed anyway.)**	[1]
3b	book again / make another appointment	[1]
4a	skiing / slalom / downhill skiing **(You can be very generous here with your spelling as long as your attempt sounds similar (e.g. skeeing, slarlem). However, 'sking' would not be allowed as it loses the main 'ee' sound.)**	[1]
4b	must be 12 / 12 years old / 12 or over **(The following answers would not be allowed, but can you see why? 12 / 12 years / 12 years and over / at least 12 years of age.)**	[1]

[Total: 8]

Exercise 2

Answer	Marks

Living on a space station
 	
Scientists and engineers are collaborating to develop space tourism.
 	
Equipment needed for travel to the station
    A pressurised **SUIT**
    Which has a **HELMET** with a means of communication
    Special boots heavy enough to keep you from floating away
	
	[1]
	[1]

Some issues with living in space
    Many of the original problems have been solved
    With little exercise bones lose **MINERALS**
    The wasting away of **MUSCLES** can be a problem
    Not experiencing a simulator means some people may get motion sickness
	
	[1]
	[1]

Food preparation and eating meals
    A meal tray is used to position the various different foods in containers
    Without the tray food could **FLOAT AWAY**
    In addition to forks, knives and spoon, **SCISSORS** are needed
	
	[1]
	[1]

Sleeping arrangements
    No space for separate cabins
    The bunks are **ATTACHED** to the walls
	
	[1]

Holiday features
    Fans, blankets, sheets and pillows
    A space walk, but not further than **10 METRES**
	
	[1]

[Total: 8]

Exercise 3

Speaker	Letter	Answer	Marks
Speaker 1	F	This is because the speaker mentions the age factor in the monologue.	[1]
Speaker 2	C	This speaker dismisses age as being an issue.	[1]
Speaker 3	A	The clue here is 25% of 18–24 year olds missing their breakfasts.	[1]
Speaker 4	E	This is because of the reference to people working in coffee shops and depending on their modern devices to carry out the work.	[1]
Speaker 5	D	This is because this speaker feels that the overloading is due to the way some people are spending their time away from the technology.	[1]
Speaker 6	G	The clue here is the reference in the monologue to being at the gym while also working and keeping your brain active.	[1]

Statement B is not relevant because none of the speakers mention food in such a specific way. There is only one reference to breakfast and it was about missing it, rather than eating the wrong type of breakfast.

[Total: 6]

Exercise 4

Question	Content answer	Marks
a	B = It measures variations in a person's DNA.	[1]
b	C = advise you that you may have an infection.	[1]
c	A = capture one year of data.	[1]
d	B = it carries out checks on an on-going basis.	[1]
e	C = getting a set amount of data.	[1]
f	A = predict diabetes in a person.	[1]
g	B = It can save them money.	[1]
h	C = it will need to be made secure on other devices.	[1]

[Total: 8]

Exercise 5

Part A

Answer	Marks

The production and uses of the salt:
    To remove ice and **SNOW** from roads
    On a daily basis 15 000 tonnes are mined
    Half a million tonnes are stored above ground
	[1]

Alternative uses for the salt mine:
    A storage business
    To store items which require a constant, cool temperature
    Currently housing 2.8 **MILLION BOXES**
    National film archives are stored in the chambers
    Some geological **ROCK SAMPLES** are stored in the tunnels
    The next James Bond film will use the tunnels for a car chase
	[1]
	
	[1]

How the salt is extracted:
    Machines powered by electricity take out walls of rock salt
    The rock salt is conveyed to the **SURFACE** where it is crushed
    25% of the rock salt is left to support the new roofs
    A **LIQUID PRODUCT** is added to stop the salt binding
	[1]
	
	[1]

An interesting fact: The word *salary* comes from Roman soldiers who used their money to buy salt.	

[Total: 5]

Exercise 5

Part B

Question	Content answer	Marks
(a)	Kristen was more interested in the **CAR CHASE** than anything else.	[1]
(b)	Renaldo said that the tunnels were **LONGER** than the local racing circuit.	[1]
(c)	Renaldo suggests that their college **PROJECT** could be carried out at the mine.	[1]
(d)	Kristen thinks that the tunnels will contain some **RARE SAMPLES** of rocks.	[1]
(e)	Both students agree that some **COURT RECORDS** might also be inside the boxes.	[1]

[Total: 5]

Pg 50-5T

Paper 1: Reading and writing

Exercise 1

Question	Answer	Marks
a	<u>written</u> guidelines	[1]
b	lack of (neighbourhood) <u>recreational</u> spaces	[1]
c	eat a <u>variety</u> of plant-based and animal-based food	[1]
d	muscles AND cardiovascular system **(BOTH REQUIRED FOR ONE MARK.)**	[1]
e	number of tasks performed by machines has risen	[1]
f	(strong) social relationships/volunteering/social activities	[1]
g	people with chronic insufficient sleep/people who sleep less than six hours a night	[1]
h	health care <u>knowledge</u>/health care <u>practices</u>	[2]
	personal planning/good lifestyle choices **(TWO REQUIRED FOR TWO MARKS.)**	
i	the environment (accept examples)	[4]
	advances in medicine	
	physical exercise	
	sleep	
	healthy diet	
	social structure	
	health science/health programmes **(ANY FOUR FROM THE ABOVE, ONE MARK EACH.)**	

[Total: 13]

Exercise 2

Question	Answer	Marks
a	D	[1]
b	B	[1]
c	A	[1]
d	C	[1]
e	C	[1]
f	A	[1]
g	A	[1]
h	B	[1]
i	D	[1]
j	A	[1]

[Total: 10]

Exercise 3

Here are some points to include, which could earn you up to 9 marks.

Heading	Answer	Marks
The sequence of activities during the family class	(a) dancing to music	[1]
	(b) stretching exercises	[1]
	(c) animal game	[1]
	(d) mat-dragging game	[1]
	(e) free running practice	[1]
	Maximum for this section 4	
Effects of the class activities on adults	(f) increase energy output	[1]
	(g) dripping with sweat	[1]
	(h) out of breath	[1]
	(i) sit exhausted in corners at break times	[1]
	(j) stimulate enthusiasm	[1]
	(k) motivated by excitement and variety	[1]
	Maximum for this section 5	

[Total: 9]

Exercise 4

Content

Here are some points to include about the content, which could earn you up to 8 marks.

Point	Content answer	Marks
1	chance to explore the limits of ability	[1]
2	the challenge of a different environment	[1]
3	the idea of living for the moment	[1]
4	distracts from the pressures of modern life	[1]
5	discover who you are	[1]
6	feeling of deep meditation	[1]
7	experience a sense of freedom	[1]
8	take control of own lives	[1]

[Total: 8]

Language

You can also get up to 8 marks for language. Use the self-assessment checklist to check your progress. If you can, show your work to your teacher.

Exercises 5 and 6: For exercises 5 and 6, you will be awarded a mark out of 16. Use the self-assessment grids to mark your answers. If you can, show your work to your teacher.

Paper 2: Listening

Exercise 1

Question	Answer	Marks
1a	the swimming pool / the pool / swimming	[1]
1b	<u>after</u> 2 months / <u>over</u> 2 months	[1]
2a	26 / twenty-six	[1]
2b	(a few) scratches / (it is) scratched **(Do not accept 'damaged' as the meaning is not precise enough.)**	[1]
3a	the <u>French</u> restaurant / the <u>new</u> restaurant / (to) eat out **(Do not accept 'to town' as it is not precise enough.)**	[1]
3b	<u>tough</u> morning / <u>tough</u> work / (a bit) tired **(Accept close spellings for tough, e.g. tuff, tuph.)**	[1]
4a	(have) blood test / give blood sample **(Do not accept 'give blood' as this has a different meaning – i.e. to do*nate* blood. It's clear she is there for a medical reason.)**	[1]
4b	(main) reception **(Do not accept pathology department as we don't know this for sure.)**	[1]

[Total: 8]

Exercise 2

Answer	Marks

The Shanghai Eye Hospital
 	
A team at the hospital has been carrying out research for a new treatment to restore lost vision.
 	
The hospital
    Specialises in eye treatment
    One of **7 / SEVEN** eye research hospitals in China
	[1]

Treatment for patients with cataracts
    Recent breakthrough in cataract cases in children
    Over 50% of cases in children **WITH BLINDNESS** are caused by cataracts
    A cataract is when the lens of the eye becomes cloudy
    Current treatment uses an **ARTIFICIAL** lens
    A tiny **CUT / INCISION** removes the cataract
    Stem cells are then added to help rebuild the lens
	[1]
	
	[1]
	[1]

Tests and trials
    Started with children
    A child's eye is likely to **REGENERATE** faster than an adult eye
    Adult trial will involve **1400 PATIENTS** lasting two years
    A smaller trial group will focus on **DIABETIC** patients
	[1]
	[1]
	[1]

Other planned research Exploring a relationship with hospitals in specialising in other eye conditions	

Schedule for the day
    Tour of the hospital facilities
    Demonstration in the **LENS LAB**
    Meet ten very special patients
	[1]

[Total: 8]

Exercise 3

Speaker	Letter	Answer	Marks
Speaker 1	E	The clue here is the <u>main</u> reason, which is relaxation.	[1]
Speaker 2	A	Notice how adventurous has been used to replace 'active'.	[1]
Speaker 3	F	Local culture is the same as to 'appreciate the local area'.	[1]
Speaker 4	B	The clue here is *climate*. This is the only speaker who specifically mentions that colder weather seems to add to the calmness and peacefulness – in the Arctic.	[1]
Speaker 5	G	This is the only speaker who talks about working while away on holiday. While other speakers *imply* that a holiday refreshes you, Speaker G is quite clear about the holidays being planned specifically for work.	[1]
Speaker 6	C	The clue is that this speakers focuses on holidays in cities and uses trains, buses, which will be noisy and busy.	[1]

Statement D is not relevant because none of the speakers mention travelling alone as opposed to travelling with others (e.g. family). When they use 'I' it doesn't mean they are alone – that is an inference you have made. Speaker 4 is the only speaker who mentions 'we'. You could infer more safely that Speaker 5 is probably on his/her own, as he/she is working, but for Speaker 5 it is clear that Statement G is much more appropriate.

[Total: 6]

Exercise 4

Question	Content answer	Marks
a	B = 1977	[1]
b	C = approximately 764 million dollars	[1]
c	A = computer graphics	[1]
d	C = They feed on electrical energy.	[1]
e	B = it was an idea that the maker of Star Wars had.	[1]
f	B = They get to travel in a *Star Wars* space craft.	[1]
g	C = Lim has been to only one theme park, but they also exist around the world.	[1]
h	A = colourful and lively.	[1]

[Total: 8]

Exercise 5

Part A

Answer	Marks

The development of the fitness park
    The aim was to provide a free facility for the people in the city
    It took **THREE YEARS** to construct the park
    The plot of land was vacant for many years
	[1]

Problems to resolve
    It was usually covered with weeds, bamboo and other flora
    It was necessary to **RELOCATE** breeds of snake
    Continued neglect meant the park was usually overgrown
	[1]

Funding the new fitness park
    An investment group proposed building **A HOTEL**
    The city council agreed to the fitness park idea
    Funds were provided by **LOCAL** **BUSINESSES**
	[1]
	
	[1]

Specialist considerations
    Excavation experts needed to make sure the ground was solid
    Architects were brought in to design the standing buildings
    A membrane was used to **PROTECT** the gym equipment
	[1]

Other uses of the park Events and gatherings where people can meet and enjoy food and drink	

[Total: 5]

Exercise 5

Part B

Question	Content answer	Marks
(a)	Jason is happy that they didn't go to the **MARKET**.	[1]
(b)	Jason thinks that **TOURISTS** will find the fitness park enjoyable.	[1]
(c)	Anita thinks that governments should ensure that local people **BENEFIT** from building projects in cities.	[1]
(d)	The two agree that not allowing **PETS** is likely to be a cultural matter.	[1]
(e)	It would seem that one of the rules is aimed at **PROTECTING** local food sellers.	[1]

[Total: 5]

Paper 1: Reading and writing

Exercise 1

Question	Answer	Marks
a	had ambition to create the world's first computer-animated films	[1]
b	criticised each other's work	[1]
c	humans were difficult to create in animated form	[1]
d	toys with different personalities who become friends	[1]
e	found him mean and unpleasant	[1]
	supposed to be the most popular toy	[1]
f	produce something good, if not better	[1]
g	every other year	[1]
h	lack new content	[1]
i	*Toy Story* a cowboy and a spaceman	[4]
	Ratatouille a rat	
	UP an old man and a boy scout	
	WALL-E a rubbish crushing robot	
	(BOTH FILM AND CHARACTER REQUIRED FOR ONE MARK.)	

[Total: 13]

Exercise 2

Question	Answer	Marks
a	B	[1]
b	D	[1]
c	A	[1]
d	C	[1]
e	A	[1]
f	B	[1]
g	A	[1]
h	C	[1]
i	D	[1]
j	C	[1]

[Total: 10]

Exercise 3

Here are some points to include, which could earn you up to 9 marks.

Heading	Answer	Marks
Duties of the snake catchers	(a) wrap snakes around statue	[1]
	(b) carry the statue through the streets	[1]
	(c) grab snakes with bare hands behind the neck	[1]
	(d) keep snakes safe before the festival	[1]
	(e) pick up fallen snakes	[1]
	(f) prevent snakes covering face and eyes of statue	[1]
	Maximum for this section 5	
Festival attractions	(g) fireworks / explosions	[1]
	(h) marching band	[1]
	(i) mobile shops selling cakes and bread	[1]
	(j) stalls selling souvenirs	[1]
	(k) choral music	[1]
	(l) festival parade	[1]
	Maximum for this section 4	

[Total: 9]

Exercise 4

Content

Here are some points to include about the content, which could earn you up to 8 marks.

Point	Content answer	Marks
1	high altitude sickness or vomiting	[1]
2	fluid accumulation in the lungs	[1]
3	hallucinations	[1]
4	frostbite / body parts become black and useless	[1]
5	lack of oxygen kills brain cells	[1]
6	sunlight burns eyes / burns corneas	[1]
7	severe physical exhaustion	[1]
8	hypothermia / severe drop in body temperature	[1]

[Total: 8]

Language

You can also get up to 8 marks for language. Use the self-assessment checklist to check your progress. If you can, show your work to your teacher.

Exercises 5 and 6: For exercises 5 and 6, you wll be awarded a mark out of 16. Use the self-assessment grids to mark your answers. If you can, show your work to your teacher.

Paper 2: Listening

Exercise 1

Question	Answer	Marks
1a	6 / six	[1]
1b	individual (interviews) / fewer people / 6 not 20 **(Do not use more than three words.)**	[1]
2a	21 degrees C / 21 deg C / 21 Celsius / 21 degrees **(The number 21 on its own would not be allowed.)**	[1]
2b	12cm **(Note that 7 + 12 = 19 is incorrect.)**	[1]
3a	2334	[1]
3b	a <u>doctor's</u> certificate **(Just putting 'certificate' is not enough here. Be careful also as 'certificate from a doctor' would lose the mark because it is too many words. If you just put 'doctor' this would also be wrong as it is the wrong idea.)**	[1]
4a	her (old) age / (her) advancing years / old age	[1]
4b	<u>low carb</u> diet **(Do not accept make the cat 'more active' as the medicine will do that. You might have put 'improve the diet', but this would not be allowed as it is not specific. The <u>low carb</u> is required.)**	[1]

[Total: 8]

Exercise 2

Answer	Marks
Shoukara's early life Graduated from university with a **LAW DEGREE** in Canada Parents were living in Canada due to their work Shoukara moved to her current home when she was **24 / TWENTY FOUR**	[1] [1]
Shoukara's early career Preferred criminal rights law due to the lack of **EQUALITY** in society Joined a law firm called *Free the world* Worked mostly as a **DEFENCE** lawyer	[1] [1]
Recollections about being a judge Was 52 when appointed as a judge Main qualities needed were speaking less and **PATIENCE / OBSERVING** Lived in special quarters during a case Was told not to discuss her work when she was at home Was once driven around in a **BULLET PROOF** vehicle Favourite court was number 4 because it is the oldest Court 4 has 80 figures of previous High Court judges and a gold desk The problem with Court 4 was that it was **COLD**	[1] [1] [1]
The purpose of her talk To focus on three interesting cases: 1) her most challenging one 2) the case which attracted the **MOST ATTENTION / MOST FUSS** 3) the case which she found the funniest	[1]

[Total: 8]

Exercise 3

Speaker	Letter	Answer	Marks
Speaker 1	A	This speaker was following the wrong career path when studying history and so changed plans to become a cook.	[1]
Speaker 2	E	This speaker is the only one who mentions smiling/ laughing at work.	[1]
Speaker 3	B	This speaker focuses on manual labour, working as a mechanic, and how repairing cars is important for many people.	[1]
Speaker 4	F	This speaker is self-employed, manages their own time and decides who to work for.	[1]
Speaker 5	C	None of the other speakers is so clear about planning for a life-long career.	[1]
Speaker 6	D	The only speaker to talk both positively and negatively about their work.	[1]

Statement G is not relevant because none of the speakers mention financial rewards.

[Total: 6]

Exercise 4

Question	Content answer	Marks
a	C = lie down and move less **(This is the only factual response. A and B are what humans think, but the only evidence is of C.)**	[1]
b	B = building trust by taking time and repeating tasks **(There is no mention of freedom (in A) and tigers bonding with each other (in C).)**	[1]
c	C = be firm **(The word 'firm' is a synonym for 'rough'. It makes sense to be careful (answer A), but you have inferred this. It was not suggested by Somchai. The relevant detail you need to locate and retrieve is C.)**	[1]
d	A = adults can spend time with all tigers **(Only answer A is correct here. If you listen carefully, B and C are actually wrong and contradicted by what Somchai says.)**	[1]
e	B = sleep for much of the day **(There are two clues. Notice that answers A and C have been worded such that they *seem* to be valid and could be true, but there is no evidence and the gist is such that tigers do not tend to be lively.)**	[1]
f	C = Everywhere. **(Answer A is incorrect and answer B has no factual evidence, so is an inference too far.)**	[1]
g	C = being home to six breeding pairs of Indo Chinese tigers **(Only answer C has the necessary detail, while answers A and B might be true they do not relate specifically to the conservation of species under threat of extinction.)**	[1]
h	A = grown steadily to 212 tigers in three compounds **(It is important to recognise that Somchai regards the growth as sensible, therefore the gist of his statement is that there has been steady growth. Note that answer C has an incorrect detail, otherwise it would also be correct.)**	[1]

[Total: 8]

Exercise 5

Part A

Answer	Marks

The history and aims of the festival
    Has been running for 15 years
    Range of international artists will be displaying their light art
    The art can be seen on buildings, landmarks and in the **STREETS /**
LOCAL NEIGHBOURHOODS
	[1]

Tourism and its impact on the city
    Two million visitors requiring around 275 000 **HOTEL ROOMS**
    1.8 billion social media 'hits'
    Festival is in the top ten listing for public outdoor events
	[1]

Highlights of this year's event
    An educational light **LAB** called *Learning in the dark*
    Session on night photography
    Talks and workshops available across the city
 	
(If you put 'workshop' this isn't correct as a lab is not the same as a workshop.)
	[1]

Providing the supply of electricity
    For the event the electricity demand rises by 300%
    Powerful **GENERATORS** are placed around the city
    Power needed only in the evenings, from 7pm to midnight
 	
(Remember your spelling of 'generators' can be a little out as long as the same number of syllables are there (4) and your spelling sounds close when pronounced out loud.)
	[1]

Next steps
    To expand and hold festivals in other countries
    The Berlin team to act as **CONSULTANTS**
    Interest has been shown by Luxembourg, Rio and Los Angeles
 	
(If you put 'advisers' this would be allowed as it is synonymous. Remember, if you use a word/phrase not from the recording it can't just be a close attempt (e.g. 'support staff' wouldn't be allowed here). Your words need to mean exactly the same.)
	[1]

[Total: 5]

Exercise 5

Part B

Question	Content answer	Marks
(a)	It is the **SECOND / 2ND** time Heidi has written about the festival.	[1]
(b)	The multi-coloured face display features <u>**OVER**</u> **1000** faces. **(You must use the word 'over'. If you put 'over one thousand' that would be three words. Always use numbers!)**	[1]
(c)	Video mapping is popular with **ADVERTISERS / IN ADVERTS**.	[1]
(d)	The two journalists would like to see the festival reach **NUMBER 1 / TOP SPOT** in the top ten list.	[1]
(e)	Heidi is keen to learn more about using light art in **(DOMESTIC) HOMES / HOUSES**.	[1]

[Total: 5]

Paper 1: Reading and writing

Exercise 1

Question	Answer	Marks
a	9.4 kilometres	[1]
b	it glows red	[1]
c	traditional Aboriginal and more recent English name	[1]
d	lead walking tours inform about flora and fauna retell Dreamtime stories **(ANY TWO FROM THE ABOVE, ONE MARK EACH.)**	[2]
e	deep holes across the south face	[1]
f	development of tourist facilities	[1]
g	keeping their original cultural values AND meeting the needs of tourists **(BOTH DETAILS REQUIRED FOR ONE MARK.)**	[1]
h	drop in visitor numbers	[1]
i	guided hike sunset dinner camel trek hiring a cycle **(ONE MARK FOR EACH CORRECT DETAIL.)**	[4]

[Total: 13]

Exercise 2

Question	Answer	Marks
a	A	[1]
b	D	[1]
c	C	[1]
d	B	[1]
e	D	[1]
f	A	[1]
g	C	[1]
h	C	[1]
i	B	[1]
j	B	[1]

[Total: 10]

Exercise 3

Here are some points to include, which could earn you up to 9 marks.

Heading	Answer	Marks
Facts about times and distances of the bull run	(a) 8am first rocket is set off	[1]
	(b) 20kms per hour is average speed of bulls	[1]
	(c) 875 metres to end of course	[1]
	(d) 2 minutes and 30 seconds is average time to complete the run	[1]
		Maximum for this section 3
Who the bull run is popular with	(e) Spanish generally	[1]
	(f) Foreigners	[1]
	(g) (Brave) young men	[1]
	(h) Writers and photographers	[1]
		Maximum for this section 3
Details of medical support	(i) 200 volunteers and Red Cross workers	[1]
	(j) First-aid post every 50 metres	[1]
	(k) About 20 ambulances	[1]
		Maximum for this section 3

[Total: 9]

Exercise 4

Content

Here are some points to include about the content, which could earn you up to 8 marks.

Point	Content answer	Marks
Reasons for twinning	(1) To promote friendship and understanding	[1]
	(2) Experience totally different culture	[1]
	(3) Encourage trade / form business links	[1]
	(4) Promote tourism	[1]
	(5) Learn a new language	[1]
Why some people would like to stop twinning	(6) No purpose in 21st century / not relevant in today's society	[1]
	(7) World travel more widely available	[1]
	(8) Communication links have improved / Skype and the Internet	[1]
	(9) Hard to justify spending of money	[1]
	(10) Inconsistent with free movement nowadays	[1]
At least one answer must be provided for each of the two content points		

[Total: 8]

Language

You can also get up to 8 marks for language. Use the self-assessment checklist to check your progress. If you can, show your work to your teacher.

Exercises 5 and 6: For exercises 5 and 6, you wll be awarded a mark out of 16. Use the self-assessment grids to mark your answers. If you can, show your work to your teacher.

D

Paper 2: Listening

Exercise 1

Question	Answer	Marks
1a	(she) lives close / lives close (by) / (it's) convenient **(The words 'she likes it' would not be allowed as it is not specific enough, and 'she lives close by' would not gain a mark as it is four words.)**	[1]
1b	current (account) **(Remember, you can be generous with your spelling, so 'curant' would be fine. Simply saying 'the first one' would not be specific enough.)**	[1]
2a	0.6% / .6% **(It is best to avoid writing the numbers as you may end up with 'nought point six percent' which is four words.)**	[1]
2b	contact governments **(If you put 'get message across' it isn't specific enough.)**	[1]
3a	a penalty (kick) / a football game / losing a game **(You have lots of options here, but remember to stick to three words.)**	[1]
3b	to be <u>tolerant</u> / more <u>tolerance</u> **(Putting 'fighting for rights' and 'equality' is not correct as there is no evidence that Ahmed thinks these are important today, as he only comments on being more tolerant.)**	[1]
4a	6 / six	[1]
4b	(on the) streets **(The clue is that there are 17 street parties in one month; that's one every two days!)**	[1]

[Total: 8]

Exercise 2

Answer	Marks
The Navajo nation The word 'Yazzie' means **SMALL** Navajo land covers around **27 000 <u>SQUARE</u>** miles Geographical area is larger than 10 of the 50 states	[1] [1]
The Navajo language Used to come up with a **<u>SECRET</u> CODE** during the war Current government conducts some of its duties using Navajo language	[1]
The Navajo economy Needs to support a population of a quarter of a million people Finding **OIL** about a hundred years ago created early wealth In 1923 a tribal government was established Most sophisticated form of American Indian government The Navajo council has 88 members serving **110** separate communities	[1] [1]
The Navajo government buildings The chambers feature vivid **<u>WALL</u> PAINTINGS** showing aspects of history An organised tour can be arranged via main office in Arizona	[1]
The Navajo Times newspaper Provided **FREE / NO COST** to the Navajo people Features story about success of the women's wrestling team Features a new education project with a nearby university All Star Awards Ceremony taking place at **SUNSET RANCH**	[1] [1]

[Total: 8]

Exercise 3

Speaker	Letter	Answer	Marks
Speaker 1	**D**	This speaker is aware of global issues, but clearly wants to prioritise issues at home.	[1]
Speaker 2	**F**	This speaker's view that it is a 'duty' is implied in a few phrases, such as *raising awareness and spread the wealth*.	[1]
Speaker 3	**A**	This speaker is clear that just one mechanism – providing money – is fraught with potential problems (corruption) and therefore argues for a range of approaches.	[1]
Speaker 4	**E**	This speaker feels that the world will be split into four or five independent power bases, which is contrary to globalisation.	[1]
Speaker 5	**G**	This speaker feels that people are currently restricted by political matters and once these are removed globalisation can really develop.	[1]
Speaker 6	**B**	This is the only speaker who talks of a fresh start, on a new planet!	[1]

Statement C is not as relevant because none of the speakers talk directly about a solution based on one nation being prominent. You can infer that Speaker 3 and Speaker 6 are probably thinking along these lines, but there is insufficient concrete evidence in what they actually say.

[Total: 6]

Exercise 4

Question	Content answer	Marks
a	B = useful, along with other resources **(Option C is interesting as the distractor because it seems to make sense, but Jane is suggesting early on that the accuracy of history books is being challenged.)**	[1]
b	B = oral stories, art and older films **(The answer is B because Jane doesn't say anything about older cultures and is actually avoiding written drafts of oral stories in her Kazakhstan project.)**	[1]
c	A = allow the reader to navigate how he or she wants to **(If you suggested C then this is an inference too far. Jane isn't explicit about wanting to reduce the impact of history books; she just wants to spend time exploring alternatives. Also, there's no indication that interactive books sell more copies.)**	[1]
d	C = facts, but not as much as people **(Jane makes it clear she wants to focus on *people* and learning more about how they lived, rather than any factual details. However, she does appreciate that facts are useful too.)**	[1]
e	B = both operate in the same way when they are working **(The answer has to be B. Option A is clearly wrong because Jane says historians are interpreters, and C isn't mentioned – i.e. making mistakes along the way, even if it is reasonable to assume that both historians and detectives will make mistakes.)**	[1]
f	A = reinventing history **(Option A is correct as the word 'reinventing' is synonymous with 'rewriting'. Historians do revisit history, but that alone is not doctoring, so B is only partly correct. The word 'reliving' (in C) implies doing things a different way, but not necessarily. Also, 'reliving' is not purposefully modifying, so it has a very different shade of meaning.)**	[1]
g	C = as avoidable **(The clue here is when Jane says 'it really doesn't have to be this way', so in other words these patterns are indeed avoidable.)**	[1]
h	B = lived in a similar way to how most people live today **(Option A is wrong. While C, though quite believable, is not soundly evidenced in anything Jane says. Although you could infer that with their violent, corrupt leaders they struggled to lead ordinary lives, but this would be an inference too far.)**	[1]

[Total: 8]

Exercise 5

Part A

Answer	Marks

The location of the community
    A hilly region in the south of France
    Temperate climate and **FERTILE LAND**
	[1]

The farm
    Is about 250 acres in size
    Requires about **20 PEOPLE** to run efficiently
    Does not make a profit
    Aims to show that self-sufficiency can help the wider community
	[1]

The goat herd
    Goats are cunning and agile
    The goats escaped and ate **POISONOUS PLANTS**
    Juliette learned that animals don't always eat sensibly
 	
(If you decided to use 'toxic' instead of 'poisonous' this is fine as it is synonymous.)
	[1]

Other challenges faced
    Lost a potato crop due to blight
    Having to repair worn-out plumbing
    Maintaining the **TRACTORS** as they are old
 	
(If you put 'machinery' this would be allowed as this is a note rather than a sentence, so grammatical accuracy is not as critical.)
	[1]

Volunteers
    Find out about the farm on the Internet
    Join for **6 WEEKS** only
    Provide unpaid work in exchange for an experience
 	
(If you put 'short time' it would not be allowed as it is not specific enough.)
	[1]

[Total: 5]

Exercise 5

Part B

Question	Content answer	Marks
(a)	Leela is reconsidering because she doesn't want to work on **(RUSTY) <u>OLD</u>** plumbing and machines. **(If you put 'worn out' this would not be fully accurate as there's no indication that the machines are actually worn out (just old and rusty).)**	[1]
(b)	The experience has encouraged Demetri to think about a **CAREER** in agriculture. **(If you put 'job' this would be fine.)**	[1]
(c)	Demetri's hobby is to fix **MACHINES / ENGINES / LATHES**. **(Don't accept 'moving parts' as these might be fine and don't need fixing.)**	[1]
(d)	Leela has decided that she would prefer **CITY** life. **(If you put 'urban' life or anything synonymous with city this would be allowed.)**	[1]
(e)	They both feel that the self-sufficiency groups in California are **<u>MORE</u> ADVANCED / <u>MORE</u> SPECIALISED**. **(Don't accept 'making things' or 'manufacturing' as this is factual and is not being questioned.)**	[1]

[Total: 5]

....

....

....

....

....

....

....

....

....

....

....

....

....

....

....

....

....

....

....

....

....

....

....

....

....

....

....

....

....

....

....

....

....

....

....

....

....

....

....

....

....

....